AF253421

The Downtown Underground

A memoir
of my time
with
the underground
drag queens of
Downtown Los Angeles

London Alexander

Some of the names of characters and other identifying
features have been changed. Some of the characters and events
are composites of people and experiences.
As always, people will have differing perspectives of the same
events—especially drag queens—and
they will not be afraid to let you know.

For Israel,

who showed me
people can change.
Without him,
I would still be
searching for home.

CONTENTS

THE
DOWNTOWN UNDERGROUND

PROLOGUE

We were running through the narrow streets of Downtown Los Angeles. The ominous summer moon lingered above us somewhere beyond the polluted haze of the city. Skid Row was littered with people forgotten by society. It was always comical the way media portrayed Los Angeles—a city of angels and movie stars, glitz and glamour, refined beauty and elegance. My boots smashed through a heaping mound of human feces.

We finally stopped at an intersection to catch our breaths. I shot a look behind us to make sure the homeless man that was giving chase gave up on his pursuit.

Pinché Queen led me toward an unmarked door. I pulled my leather jacket tightly around my neck to warm my nerves rather than my body. We entered. The lights were dim—making it almost impossible to see. I reached for Pinché, but the only thing in my hand was a dense fog.

I wandered around blind and alone.

A maniacal cackle reverberated from the corner. Meatball stared at me with a deranged grin. He heaved with laughter with every step I took, as if he knew my fate before it was written.

I shoved my way through a crowd, bumping into monsters like Vander Von Odd, Frankie Doom, and Xochi Mochi. I was a lost child in a twisted nightmare, staring up at towering drag queens clad in tight leather and gritty makeup. The lack of elegance was made up for with terror. Beauty was replaced with a calculated ugliness. The desire to fit a mold was broken by the need to innovate.

I raced ahead only to stop abruptly. A sea of discarded pieces lay before me. An angelic figure emerged from the shadows. Ali Doom exerted a siren's song. I was mesmerized—ready to follow her to the end of the world.

She defiantly blazed a path through the broken pieces. I gazed at the potential around me. The rejected scraps were unique—there was something special about them.

My fixation was shattered. I continued through the labyrinth of horror until I reached a deteriorating gate. In front of it stood the Haus of D'vil. Saint Peter D'vil reigned as the gatekeeper. Nobody was allowed to pass without first paying their respects. I bowed to the fang necklace forged by the godmother of the alternative world.

I made my way through the gate into the courtyard. In front of me stood a celestial monster known as Ursula. The drag queen swayed to a melancholy melody. His colossal height wrecked the heavens above. Across his stomach the word 'FAGGOT' was scarred. He licked his lips, raising a staple gun to his head. A flux of staples collided with his face. Again. And again. And again. Blood gushed down his body.

Watching above from dueling thrones were the Boulet Brothers. They applauded the art. They offered a platform to the discarded. They welcomed the broken. Next to them stood Tito—the embodiment of queer nobility. He held the key to everlasting acceptance, willing to present it to anyone wishing to enter.

I stood below them, allowing the Stockholm Syndrome to

caress me in the nightmare. This was a world that welcomed the freaks, the outcasts, and all the strange kids that never believed they belonged. It was a place for anyone that didn't fit a mold. This was a home that welcomed all the queers that didn't fit in with the rest of society.

This was the Downtown Underground.

PART I

FOUR LOKOS, ECSTASY, AND DINOSAURS

I had finally turned eighteen and everything in my life was coming together. I had just graduated as the valedictorian of my High School; I was on my way to a prestigious university on a full-ride scholarship; and I volunteered my free time reading to blind children.

Actually, none of that was true.

I was sitting on the gravel of a parking lot, next to broken glass and stale piss, chugging a Four Loko somewhere in Southern California's Inland Empire. Next to me was my impressively butch friend, Dani, draining a can of her own. Between each sip of the energy-packed malt beer, our eyes darted around to make sure there were no security guards patrolling the area.

We were just outside of a gay nightclub that was privy to underage drinking. Being the only club in the county that allowed eighteen-year-olds to enter, we didn't want to spoil our chances of getting in. However, that didn't stop us from making questionable decisions.

"The grape flavor is so good," Dani said.

"I don't even care that it's warm," I agreed. "I wonder why they call it 'black out in a can'."

"Probably because some dumb kids didn't know their limits and drank too much." She finished her Four Loko before cracking open another.

I pulled a little plastic bag out of my pocket. In it was two white pills with the imprint of a dolphin on them.

"You think it's a bad idea if we take one?" I asked.

"What is it?" Dani replied.

"Ecstasy."

"Aren't you not supposed to roll while drinking?"

"Probably."

I tossed the pill into my mouth. Dani tapped her Four Loko against mine.

"Cheers."

I could feel the bitter white dolphin swimming around in a malted grape euphoria. We finished our cans and tossed them into a corner of the parking lot. A hollow clank resonated as they collided with discarded bottles from other underage drinkers. We reached the line to the club just in time for the 10 o'clock deadline for free entry.

As I stood waiting to enter, I caught a glimpse of myself in the reflection of a window. I adjusted my swooping emo-style jet-black hair, smoothed out my deep purple V-neck, and realigned the smearing black eyeliner on my face. 2009 was in full effect, and I was living for every minute of it.

"So hot," I whispered to myself, pouting my lips.

I scanned everyone in the line around me, wondering how many of them were going to hit on me that night. The Inland Empire had a very simple crowd even for a gay venue. There were butch lesbians with tattooed eyebrows, guys wearing baggy jeans, and everyone wore basic T-shirts.

They all retained the same scowls across their faces. Breaking the stereotype of gays being friendly, you would find yourself in a confrontation instantly if you looked at someone in the I.E. the wrong way.

"See anything good?" Dani asked.

"Not yet," I replied. "I better hookup tonight, though.

Otherwise going out is pointless.”

After I flashed a flirtatious smile to the security guard checking my I.D., I entered a club for the first time. The place was massive. The dance floor dominated the room just below the DJ's booth. A small stage barely rose above the floor at the top of the venue. On the opposite end was a lounge area.

“Holy balls!” I shouted at Dani. “This is incredible!”

My virgin eyes soaked in the atmosphere. I had never seen so many gay people together in one place. Guys were grinding on each other on the dance floor. Girls were making out in corners. My little queer heart was about to burst with happiness. Although, it could have just been the Four Loko and drugs mixing together.

“C'mon, we have to request a song,” Dani said, leading me to the DJ's booth.

Convenient slips of paper and pens rested on top of the booth, welcoming anyone to leave a request. Dani wrote her song while I took a handful of papers and abused the system: “Miley Cyrus—Party in the U.S.A.”, “Miley Cyrus—Party in the U.S.A.”, “Miley Cyrus—Party in the U.S.A.”

My musical taste had transformed drastically from High School. I had met my first gay friend a few months prior, and I was on a crash course of queer culture. I traded in listening to Marilyn Manson, Bowie, and The Germs to learn about Madonna, Britney Spears, and what a power bottom was.

I feverishly wrote down ‘Miley Cyrus’ one more time when my attention was diverted to a broad-shouldered woman gliding past me. She was over six feet tall with a toned body. Her face was covered in makeup, giving her a soft complex, but her eyebrows were jagged, leaving a cold demeanor.

Her straight, black hair brushed against her back muscles as she moved toward the stage. Her heels clicked against the stairs. Her thick hands grasped a microphone.

“Welcome, all you homos,” her deep voice boomed into the mic. “Are you all ready for a show? My name is Raven and, I hate to disappoint you, but I am not actually a real woman. I am, however, your hostess for the evening.”

A few pitiful applause rose from the audience.

"They do shows at clubs?" I asked Dani. "That's stupid. I just want to dance."

"It will be over soon—hopefully," Dani replied.

Raven made a feeble attempt to entertain the audience when Dani escorted me to the lounge area opposite the stage. Sitting in a dilapidated booth was a round, meek looking boy with thick-rimmed glasses.

"This is my friend, Israel," Dani introduced him.

"Hi!" I shouted, excited to add another queer person to my homosexual Pokédex.

"Hey," Israel responded with a high-pitched voice.

"Why are you sitting in the corner by yourself?"

"Just watching the show." Israel sipped his water. He pushed his glasses up, turning his attention back to the stage.

"I know what you're all thinking," Raven continued. "You're thinking, 'damn, drag queens are so glamorous. They must be making a ton of money'."

"Doesn't he mean 'cross-dresser'?" I asked.

"Girl, just watch," Israel replied.

Raven continued, "Sure, we may look stunning with our shimmering jewelry and our sleek gowns, but do you see this?" He pulled off his diamond bracelet. He held it up for the audience to see the spotlight gleaming off it. "I actually made this myself. Beautiful isn't it? I'll let you in on a little secret. I took an empty roll of masking tape and glued rhinestones onto it."

Genuine laughter emitted from the audience.

"Oh, you don't believe me?" Raven squeezed the malleable bracelet between two of his fingers before it returned to its shape.

The audience erupted.

"Bitch, I'm poor. Dressing like a woman doesn't pay the bills. We call this 'ballin' on a budget'. But enough of that, let's get to the show."

Raven tossed the microphone aside as music replaced his voice. He glided around the stage, moving his arms and lips to the lyrics of the song. He wasn't quite dancing. He certainly wasn't actually singing. But somehow, the audience was captivated—especially Israel.

"What's going on?" I asked.

"Look at how good he is!" Israel exclaimed. He moved his hands in the same flowing manner as the drag queen. He silently sang along to the pop song without removing his eyes from the performance.

"He's just pretending to sing," I whined. "And walking around. This is weird. When can we—"

My hand gripped the center of my chest. My heart slammed against my body with a sharp beat. My eyes widened. A smile stretched across my face.

"Whoa."

"What happened?" Dani asked.

"Are you okay?" Israel followed.

My heart rate doubled. My jaw clenched. My eyes absorbed every particle of light around me.

"Do you feel it?!" I asked.

"Feel what? The Loko?" Dani replied.

"No, the ecstasy."

"I didn't take one. Did you take a pill?"

"What the hell? I thought you were taking one with me!"

"I told you, you're not supposed to drink while rolling!"

"Fuck."

Raven concluded his performance just as I was realizing I might die. The DJ finally opened the dance floor with Beyonce's "Diva".

"Oh my god, let's go dance!" I yanked Dani and Israel.

"No, no, no..." Israel protested. "I'm not going out there in front of all those people."

"What? Why? Fine. Let's go, Dani."

I pulled her toward the dance floor beneath the strobe lights. The fog machines engulfed us.

Within minutes, my entire body was drenched with sweat. Like the queer, drug-fueled version of the movie Speed, I thought I would die if I didn't keep moving. As the DJ cycled through songs for the next hour, I kept up with all of them. I grinded on strangers; I did the Jerk; I taught people how to Dougie; and I rapped to Pitbull.

I danced between a middle-aged woman and her girlfriend. My body was full of love and energy. I tried to kiss them. Dani pulled me back to the other side of the dance floor before anyone could punch me. I leaned against her and bent over in a gruesome attempt to twerk.

I caught a glimpse of my reflection in a mirror. I wiped my bangs away from my sweaty face. My hair was dripping wet. There was no doubt that my eyeliner was somewhere around my chin. I continued gyrating my one-hundred-ten-pound body. I felt like I was God's gift to the gay community even though my lanky body was probably moving like those inflatable tube men outside car dealerships.

I tried to focus my vision toward the people on the dance floor. "Why is nobody hitting on me?" I asked Dani.

"No idea," she replied, politely.

"I think I need some water."

Dani got lost dancing with a woman that she would probably move in with in a week because that's what lesbians did when they had the slightest bit of attraction to each other.

I swayed through the venue, winking at every person along the way. I dodged tables and chairs, heading toward the restroom. My eyes locked on the sink with tremendous effort. I turned the faucet on, sticking my head underneath. The grainy water filled my mouth, gulp after gulp. I felt like I had finally found an oasis in a dry desert.

As I was hydrating, I could feel a body approach from behind me. I felt a pair of hands grip my waist tightly. A surge of euphoria ran through my nervous system. Goosebumps rose from my cold skin. The hairs on the back of my neck stood up.

"Whoa," I said, looking behind me in the mirror.

My vision blurred, making it impossible to see the details of the person's face behind me. Their hands shifted toward the front of my body then into my pants.

I knew I was hot, I thought to myself. *This is what love feels like. This is the gay world. I've finally found a community where I fit in.*

The hands kept drifting around the inside of my jeans. I was enjoying the attention, but I wished I wasn't so incoherent.

I wanted to get back to Dani. I wanted to keep dancing, but I was stuck in the restroom with a stranger.

A beam of light bounced off the mirror, further disrupting my vision. The hands quickly slipped out of my pants; the body backed away, disappearing. I turned to see a large security guard shining their flashlight on me. I covered my enlarged pupils, slipping out of the restroom.

I stumbled through the lounge area, bumping into Israel. "Have you seen Dani?" I slurred.

"She's right there." Israel pointed to her walking up to us.

"We need to go," I said. "I don't think—"

My mouth stopped moving. I could feel it hang open, but words refused to come out. I couldn't blink. I could see everything around me. I could see Dani and Israel staring. I could see strangers coming up to us. Everything sounded the same, but I couldn't react to anything. My mind was happy, but I had no idea what expression my face was conveying.

"London, are you okay?" Israel asked.

"Are you all right?" Dani echoed.

My body stopped functioning. I was standing but couldn't move. I wanted to speak but I couldn't. My brain kept telling my body to move, but it was as if my mind couldn't send it messages. I could feel my heart race so fast that it felt like everything around me was in slow motion.

"Jesus," I finally managed to choke out. "I think I just died for a second… Let's go dance!"

"Were you just in a K-hole?" Dani asked.

I shrugged.

"Maybe you should sit down," Israel suggested.

"Maybe you should stop sitting in the corner and go enjoy yourself," I snapped back.

"Israel might be right," Dani agreed.

"Want to take another shot?" I asked, changing the subject.

"Let's do it," she replied, easily swayed.

Dani pulled out a couple of travel-sized bottles of vodka from her pockets. She took a sip then handed the 99-cent bottle to me.

"Cheers."

Just as the plastic bottle touched my lips, security surrounded us. They ripped the bottle from my hand and shoved Dani and me out of the lounge area, escorting us through the crowded venue.

"What the hell?!" Dani defiantly screamed at them.

"You guys are drinking while underage. You're out of here," the security reprimanded.

"No we weren't!" Dani protested.

Before the clock even struck midnight, my gay Cinderella story was coming to an abrupt conclusion. I looked back at the sanctuary of queer liberation while the security guard was dragging me away. Just before we reached the exit, "Party in the U.S.A." blasted from the speakers.

"Just one more song," I begged the security guard. "You can even come dance with us."

With one last impressive shove, Dani and I found ourselves back in the parking lot. We dragged ourselves through the loose gravel passed the piss I left on the side of the Thai restaurant earlier. Dani shouted every obscenity along the way, accusing the security guard of not only being racist but homophobic as well.

I tossed my keys to her.

"We can chill at my place," I said. "But you should probably drive."

Twenty minutes later, we pulled up to my parents' house. The car landed dangerously close to the bushes in the front yard. We fell out of the car and snuck around the side of the house to a room detached from the main part of the property.

I collapsed onto my bed, closing my eyes but not feeling the least bit tired. Dani paced around the room feeding into the angry lesbian stereotype.

"That place sucks anyway," she spewed. "I'm never going back."

"The one time I fit into a place, I get kicked out," I lamented. "I guess I don't belong in the gay world."

Dani's tension eased with laughter. "You think that was the gay world? That was just a bar full of drunk people."

"Yeah, but it was the only place where I've been able to be around other homos."

"You'll find somewhere to fit in."

"I guess. You should probably spend the night. There are extra shorts in the closet."

Dani rummaged through my closet of multi-colored shirts and ripped jeans while I laid in a pool of my own sweat, trying to stabilize my vision.

"What's this?" Dani asked, pulling out a small machine.

"That's still in there? It's a tattoo gun. My friend must have forgot it here when she moved out."

"Is there ink?"

I pointed to a shoebox full of tattooing accessories.

"Want a tattoo?" A sadistic smile stretched across Dani's face.

"That sounds like the worst idea right now," I said. "Let's do it."

Dani excitedly plugged the machine into the wall. She set up the foot pedal, pulled out a cartridge of black ink, and threw on some tattered gloves that looked like they had already been used.

"Wait. What are you going to tattoo?" I had almost forgot to ask.

"Hm..."

Dani grabbed a piece of paper, quickly scribbling on it. She held up the result.

"A dinosaur?" I asked.

"We can put it on your ankle," she suggested.

"I don't know. It seems really basic. I want something special."

Dani returned to sketching then held up the paper again.

"A dinosaur riding a skateboard?" I asked. "Hell yeah!"

I turned onto my side and stretched out my leg. Dani drowned the needle in ink. She gently pressed the pedal, and the machine vibrated with an intimidating sound. She placed the needle against my skin.

"It's not coming out," she said.

"Press harder."

Dani shoved the needle so far into my skin that my bones rattled. She skidded it around like scissors across wrapping paper. Blood poured from my ankle. I watched in horror as I knew I should have been in pain but couldn't feel anything.

"Okay, I think the outline is done. Now I need to shade," she announced.

"Have you ever tattooed someone before?" I asked.

"Nope."

Dani entered my skin even harder. She dragged the needle back and forth in circles, sawing through my skin. I struggled trying to see what she was doing, but she wanted to wait until the end before revealing her masterpiece. I was excited to see the birth of the ferocious creature. The vicious animal that was once at the top of the food chain would reign supreme on my skin forever.

The sound of the tattoo gun faded.

"Um, I got some bad news," Dani said. "I don't think there's going to be room for a skateboard."

"Damn," I replied. "Then it's just a basic dinosaur. What if you sign your name next to it? That way it's still special."

After a short night jammed with excess drinking, drugs, and gayness, I had a scar on my body that would commemorate the first time I got kicked out of a club. Dani stepped back to admire her work. I grimaced moving my ankle closer to my dilated pupils. I wiped away the caking blood, excited to see the majestic creature.

There was definitely a dinosaur on my ankle, but it was far from ferocious. It turned out to be more of a cross between a crooked Yoshi and a snaggletoothed Barney. It rested on its hind legs with a gimpy little arm, forever scarred on my body. Next to the animal was the signature of a girl that I had known for only a few weeks. I thanked God that at least there was no room for a skateboard.

SHIT-OH-FIVE

BEEEEEM! BEEEEEM!

I bolted up to the sound of my alarm cranking out an unholy tune. I was happy to find myself in my own bed, under my own blankets, in my own room. It wasn't every morning that I could be so lucky to recognize where I woke up.

I reached below the covers in search of the devil device that woke me. My hands brushed against a cheap polyester smoothness running along my body. I ripped the morning goo from my eyes to find myself wearing a tiny, black cocktail dress.

"Oh, come on," my dehydrated throat choked out.
I rolled out of bed like a Barbie doll unable to separate its legs too far. The dress constricted my body. My phone fell out of my bed, graciously snoozing itself. I gingerly stepped over to my mirror.

"What. The. Fuck."

The dress twisted; the straps laid horizontal like a Monday night prostitute; my eyes were matted together by old mascara; glitter covered my body. Despite the dishevel of my appearance and my soul, my hair was perfectly managed by copious amounts of hairspray.

I looked down to see a half-empty bottle of Jack Daniels laughing at me from the floor.

"You sneaky little... You got me again." I shook my finger at the coy bottle of booze.

I couldn't be mad at the little guy. Jack Daniels may have had a twisted sense of humor, but he never meant any harm. I sat down next to him with hope that the world would stop spinning so fast. I continued staring at the mirror.

I knew I was planning on wearing that dress to a party as a joke, but I couldn't remember if that party was the previous night. I assumed it was, but my memory wouldn't let me be so sure. The pounding in my head distracted me from my fragmented thoughts.

In the reflection of the mirror, I could see someone coming into my room.

"Happy Pride! Oh my god, I'm so excited! Are you, like, ready yet?!" Kristina screeched.

"Do you have to talk?"

"Whoa, you look lost."

"Well..."

Jack Daniels winked at me.

"What's with the dress?" Kristina asked.

"Actually, maybe you can tell me? Were you with me last night?"

"Nope."

"Ugh!" I collapsed onto the floor, closing my eyes.

I was only a year into my drinking career, but my liver was probably aging like a dog. My life revolved around the party nightlife which included—but was not limited to—copious amounts of alcohol, a revolving door of drugs, and never knowing what day it was.

Kristina helped me to my feet then assisted in the removal of the dress. I didn't have a clue how women were able to remove their clothes without the help of someone. Which is probably why I hadn't taken it off before passing out.

I changed into jeans and a tank top. My tiny, white arms hung out of the extra-small clothes that were still too big for me. I poured more hairspray onto my already stiff hair. The aerosol made me nauseous. Then, I maneuvered my makeup and caked on more to make it seem like I cared about being presentable to the world.

"Do we really have to go?" I cried to Kristina.

"It's your first Pride festival! I want to be the one to take you! Like, we have to go! Maybe you shouldn't have partied so hard last night."

I laid back on my bed. I had already expended what little energy I had.

"In my defense, I have no idea what happened last night," I said.

BEEEEEM! BEEEEEM!

"Goddamn it!"

I picked up my phone and put the alarm out of my misery. Then, I searched through my pictures to jog some sort of memory of the previous night's festivities. There were only a couple of pictures, but they proved that I did, in fact, wear the dress to the party.

It was a party I had known about weeks in advance. Inexplicably, one of my friends wanted to have a formal masquerade party while his parents were out of town. I refused to wear a suit and tie because my small frame made formal clothes look like a joke on me.

I didn't want to miss out on a party because of an unnecessary dress code. I decided it would be a brilliant idea to show up in a dress, both as an act of defiance against the dress code, and also because I would probably look better in a dress than a suit.

That's where my memory ended. I scrolled to a picture of my friend Piper and me wearing matching dresses just before entering the party.

"Who else are we meeting at Pride?" I asked.

"A few of my friends," Kristina answered.

"You think Piper will be there?"

"For sure."

"She'll know what happened last night."

I finally got up, fighting gravity on the way. Kristina

squealed with excitement as she stepped outside.

"But, I'm not drinking today," I declared.

I heard a faint giggle escape my room. I looked back to see Jack Daniels with a flirtatious smirk.

"Oh, Jack..."

I grabbed him by the neck and followed Kristina.

We were cruising west on Santa Monica Boulevard with the windows rolled down. Kesha blasted from the radio as puffs of smoke raced out of the car into the sizzling summer sky. I stared more into the mirror, fixing my makeup than at the road. Kristina packed us another bowl of Los Angeles' cheapest weed.

"Why are we getting nowhere?" I bellowed. The street was covered in traffic forcing me to stop the car every few feet.

"Are we even close to WeHo yet?" Kristina asked, lighting up the bowl.

"WeHo? You mean West Hollywood?"

"'WeHo' is like what everyone calls West Hollywood."

"Well, that's stupid."

My car crawled passed La Cienega. I took a hit of weed.

"Have you texted Piper yet?" I asked.

"She's probably blacked out already."

I had known Piper for only a year, but it felt like forever. Her and I were good friends that did typical friend things, like getting banned from going into the ocean by a lifeguard, or simultaneously running into a glass window, or commandeering an idle bulldozer. Then there was the time that I was carrying her, but she insisted on carrying me at the same time. Logic and gravity defeated us both. Piper fell back, jamming her skull into the corner of a wall, knocking herself out momentarily.

I stayed friends with her for a few reasons. First, she drank more than I did. No matter how trashy my life seemed, I found solace in knowing that Piper was always worse. Second, she was of drinking age and willingly offered to buy me alcohol whenever I asked.

"No response. We're going to have to find her on our own," Kristina said.

"Ugh."

We continued inching our way along the street, smoking and listening to culturally appropriate pop music like Katy Perry and Lana Del Rey. On either side of us were restaurants that were much more upscale than our usual Taco Bell destination. It was the kind of area in Los Angeles where people brought their dogs into food establishments, spas, and everywhere else where animals shouldn't have been allowed.

"Looks like we're almost there." Kristina pointed out the window.

I strained my bloodshot eyes to see two women strolling down the sidewalk, holding hands. One wore jean shorts with a red flannel tied around her waist. The other was a thicker woman wearing a deep, white V-neck and a backwards hat. The wind swept through their hair. The sun illuminated their smiles. They were glowing.

"Oh my god," I said. "They're holding hands in public and nobody is screaming at them."

"That's WeHo," Kristina replied.

"Unreal."

I had never seen a queer couple holding hands so casually with no repercussions. Whenever I went on dates with guys, I would hold their hand until we got near people. Once we got close to anyone, I would release their hand to scratch my face or adjust my hair—anything that gave my hand somewhere else to be. It was a necessary reaction to avoid having obscenities yelled at us or garbage thrown at our faces.

As a teenager, I didn't have time to think about the butterflies in my stomach or the nervousness that came with falling in love. Instead, I had to worry about adults coming up to me and screaming "faggot" in my face for reasons I never quite figured out.

That day was different, however. Kristina and I watched the two women holding hands. I was consumed with a mixture of jealousy and pride, but it also gave me hope.

The honking of a horn snapped me out of my fixation. I accelerated to keep up with traffic. We rolled to the next intersection, where I saw another female couple holding hands on the opposite sidewalk—then a male couple behind them. After a few blocks of soaking in the queer utopian street, we came across something I never believed existed: a family of two older gay men pushing a stroller with a little girl clutching a stuffed animal in it.

"Is this real life?" I asked.

"Liberating, isn't it?" Kristina replied.

We decided that we could probably walk faster than we were driving. I pulled into a gas station that was charging an absurd amount of money for parking. We gave the attendant four drinks worth of money and felt our hearts break, but we didn't have much of a choice.

We joined the pedestrians passing Larrabee Street, when the atmosphere escalated to an entirely different level. The casual crowd was replaced with men on stilts roaming around, semi-naked people covered only by shimmering glitter, and middle-aged women wearing rainbow paraphernalia from head to toe. There was even a person dressed like Jesus Christ, posing for photos.

We passed more bars in a single block than I had ever seen in an entire city. Trunks was overflowing with people; Mickey's had go-go dancers on every table; we passed Revolver and Rage; we saw a tiny bar called The Bayou tucked away across from Motherlode.

"Pride is amazing!" I told Kristina.

"This isn't even the festival yet! This is still just Santa Monica Boulevard."

We continued weaving our way in and out of the crowd. I nearly ran into a shirtless man's chiseled abs. His hard body would have shattered my face if I hadn't avoided him.

"Everyone here looks like a damn fitness model," I said to Kristina.

The majority of the guys in WeHo were either thin, blond, white guys or muscly, blond, white guys. The thin ones wore tiny thongs, and the muscled men looked like typical college athletes. It looked like Abercrombie puked all over the city, leaving spawns of nearly identical bodies.

We finally found the entrance to the festival where the

man dressed like Jesus stood. Like a queer messiah, he pointed the way. Kristina and I entered below the rainbow archway at the West Hollywood Park signifying the official L.A. Pride event.

The festival was much less impressive than the outside. There were a couple rows of booths selling merchandise or advertising various causes. Multiple dance tents rested on the outskirts. There was a small area serving food next to a large area of portable restrooms.

We wandered around collecting free samples of condoms and flavored lubricant when we heard a loud "woo!" in the distance.

"The white girl call," Kristina and I said to each other simultaneously.

We heard it again—another high-pitched "woo!". It was the sound that white girls naturally made when drinking alcohol. It was in their DNA and they couldn't help it. Like the way a dog can't help but bark even when you tell them it's okay not to. A white girl couldn't refrain from "wooing" when drinking.

We turned a corner to find exactly what we expected: Piper was chugging wine out of a plastic cup while spinning a giant wheel of prizes.

"Woo!" She screamed again. "Dick whistle, dick whistle, dick whistle!" She was frightening the man hosting the wheel. Next to Piper was a cute, slim boy with shaggy hair. Below his left eye was a horizontal black stripe, not unlike a baseball player's.

To Piper's disappointment, the wheel landed on beads instead of the plastic toy whistle in the shape of a penis. She tossed the prize around her neck and turned around. Her eyes were like two fish rapidly swimming away from each other behind her glasses. Her chin and white T-shirt were stained with the deep red of wine. However, nobody would really notice because, beneath the shirt, was a pair of D-sized breasts.

"Piper!" I yelled, even though we were two feet directly in front of her.

Her head snapped side to side searching for my voice.

"Piper!" Kristina echoed.

Finally, she noticed us. She pressed her big beaded breasts against us in a hug that was more of her falling over than actual affection.

"Dude, bro!" Piper shouted in my face. "I didn't get the dick whistle."

"It's like noon and you're already wasted?" I asked.

"You woke up in a dress," Kristina reminded me.

"You slept in a dress?" The cute boy asked me.

"Who are you?" I returned.

"Guys, this is Diego," Piper introduced. "I found him."

"I didn't want to leave her by herself," Diego clarified. "She seems like she shouldn't be left alone."

"Did you see these beads I won?" Piper asked us. "Do you want to spin the wheel? It's free and every booth has one."

"First, what happened last night?" I demanded.

"Dick whistle."

"Ok, but—"

"Dick whistle!"

"All right! Holy hell!"

For the next hour, Piper, Kristina, Diego, and I jumped from booth to booth spinning prize wheels in hopes of getting a plastic toy phallus. We each had growing bags of somewhat useful items like gym towels that had porn website logos, condoms, gummy worms, and douche bottles.

"If this is what Pride is all about, then I'm happy to be gay," I announced, grabbing a free sample of toothpaste from a booth.

"Yeah, but we didn't get the whistle," Piper reminded us for at least the hundredth time that day.

We had already spun every wheel at the event, and the booths didn't allow us to repeat spins no matter how loud Piper protested. She was spilling her wine with every step. Kristina was stoned trying to focus on putting one foot in front of the other in an attempt to walk. I was barely sobering up from the night before, which meant I could finally feel the hangover creeping in. The only person who seemed put together in our group was Diego, and we didn't even know him.

We turned down an aisle and, as if WeHo Jesus himself had illuminated the booth, there was one last wheel that we had not harassed yet.

"Me first!" Piper yelled to nobody trying to stop her.

"We've been wandering around all day," I complained, "and you still haven't told me what happened last night. Do you even remember?"

"Of course I remember." She spun the wheel with great determination. "We went to the party. I did your makeup. And hair. And painted fake cleavage on you. You know, like a girl. You wore a masquerade mask because you didn't want people to know it was you. Where did you get that mask? It was so cool."

"Focus."

"Then I 'introduced' you to Dani. She started hitting on you. So you took the mask off. That didn't stop her, though. She kept trying to put her fingers inside you. You looked like a hot woman."

"You would definitely make a hot woman," Kristina chimed in.

"You're a cute guy, though," Diego smirked, catching my attention.

"You drank Jack before we got there. Then martinis," Piper continued. "After you chugged wine out of a beer bong, someone brought out a machete. They kept swinging it around —almost hitting the other guy in a dress."

"There was another guy in a dress?" I asked.

"Yeah, but it wasn't you."

"Then what happened? How did I get home?"

"I don't know. I left after the machete. Ask Spoons."

"Spoons was there?"

"Yeah. We came here together too."

"Spoons is here?!" Kristina exclaimed.

"Why didn't you tell us?" I added.

The prize wheel was still spinning: Condom. Pen. Lube. Condom. Towel. Dick whistle. Finally, it slowed.

"Dick whistle, dick whistle, dick whistle," Piper shouted.

The wheel clicked slowly. It landed on the dick whistle slot but edged over to the next item.

"Horse shit!" Piper yelled like the lady that she was.

I handed the host five dollars and begged him to just give her the plastic toy. Either he felt bad enough for the wine-stained princess, or I overpaid for an erotic Chuck E. Cheese prize. He handed her the tiny dick. She blew into it to make an incessant whistling noise.

"Now, let's go find Spoons," I suggested.

"Who's Spoons?" Diego asked.

Kristina, Piper, and I exchanged looks.

"Have you ever seen a giant straight man twerk so hard to Britney Spears that his pants split in the middle of a dance floor?" Kristina asked.

"Have you ever met someone that has openly cried on his pancakes at Denny's so hard that a waitress offered him a hug?" Piper asked.

"Have you ever seen a six-foot-two man grind on an even larger man wearing nothing but a diaper?" I asked.

"Um, no," Diego responded.

"Then you're in for a treat."

The four of us searched around L.A. Pride for the man that a security guard once referred to as "that big dumbass". Spoons was an unpredictable free spirit, but we had a good idea of where we could find him.

First, we checked every bar at the event and, naturally, grabbed a drink at each one. Then we checked his second favorite place. We searched all around the various food trucks. Despite the aroma of SoCal tacos permeating our noses, we avoided eating as to not compromise our drunken state. We were saving money by not eating and getting even more intoxicated—a win-win.

The alcohol rapidly coursing through our bodies made it increasingly difficult to locate our friend. At that point, all we could hope for was that he still had his clothes on and hadn't got arrested yet.

The next logical places to check were the dance tents. God gifted Spoons with many attributes but shame and self-awareness were not among them. He was known to challenge every go-go dancer—male or female—to a dance battle wherever we went. He rocked his "dad bod" with unwavering confidence.

We sauntered past the tent playing country music; there was no chance of Spoons being in there. Then we got to the hip-hop tent where we really hoped that he wasn't getting low to "Bedrock" or any other Young Money song. Finally, we reached the pop-music tent.

Carly Rae Jepsen blasted from the speakers. This was more Spoons' forte than any of the previous options. The tent was packed with people, making it impossible for the four of us to stay together. Sweaty, glittery bodies separated Piper from us. Kristina tried to pull her back but got sucked into the crowd with her. Lady Gaga's Bad Romance erupted around us, eliciting a roar from the crowd.

"Oh my god, this is my song," said Diego and every other homosexual in a three-mile radius. "Let's go dance!"

"I have to find my friends," I protested.

"Just one song."

He grabbed my hand. The electricity of his touch jolted every gay hormone in my body. I couldn't pass up the chance to dance with an attractive guy at L.A. Pride while Lady Gaga serenaded us. I smiled, allowing him to lead me to the center of the dance tent.

Diego, along with everyone else beneath the tent, mouthed the words to the song. We were surrounded by hundreds of queers, and I couldn't think of any better place to be. That little bubble of gayness felt like the safest place I had ever been. I felt comfortable. I felt welcomed. I was falling in love with the moment and hoped it would never end.

Diego's body pressed against mine as personal space was becoming scarce. My heart beat with nervousness. I could feel the butterflies in my stomach, and I didn't have to worry about the judgment of straight people. Diego's glossy brown eyes stared back at me. The black stripe beneath his eye glistened. He was so alluring that I couldn't tell if I wanted to be him or if I wanted to be with him.

"Are you a top or bottom?" He asked.

"Um, what?" I responded.

"Top or bottom?"

"I'm just trying to dance right now."

Of course, I would have been very open to the idea of having sex with him eventually, but in that moment, I just wanted to revel in the euphoria of dance.

"Yeah, but you're a bottom right?" He continued.

"Actually, I'm a top."

"Oh. But you're so small."

"Um, okay?"

I could feel Diego's muscles tense as his body pulled the slightest bit away from me. I understood that our sexual preferences may not have matched up, but that didn't mean we couldn't enjoy dancing together. The DJ transitioned the song away from Lady Gaga. Suddenly, Diego found enough space to put in between us.

"It's just that tops are supposed to be tall and muscly. Nobody really goes for the smaller guys. I mean, I totally respect that you want to be a top," he said, condescendingly.

Unfortunately, we both knew that he wasn't wrong. Despite being at an event that was supposed to be accepting of everyone—despite being surrounded by hundreds of queer people—in an instant, I felt so alone.

We kept dancing but drifted further apart. We allowed more and more people to squeeze between us until we could no longer see each other. The crowd swallowed us in separate directions and neither of us stopped it.

The sun had completely set on the West Coast. Pride was transitioning into nighttime, which meant that people had been excessively drinking all day—including myself.

I escaped the pop-music tent back to the aisle of booths. People were puking all over the park. Fights were breaking out with security guards trying to pull people apart. The medical tent had a longer line of people than the bars.

I shoved my way toward the neighborhood of portable restrooms. I was waiting in line when a person cut in front of me. Regardless of how bad I had to use the facilities, I let them stay to avoid an unnecessary confrontation. As I waited, a muffled moan escaped one of the plastic restrooms.

I gazed around to see if anyone else noticed the sound of a whale being harpooned. Everyone seemed too intoxicated to notice or care. Then the door to the restroom next to me swung open. The musty air escaped the box, slamming the stench of baked summer piss into my face. My eyes watered.

Through my burning tears, I managed to see a tall man ducking out of the toilet. His feet hit the grass. He stood with pride like a man that just conquered a wild beast. Behind him was a woman that looked like she escaped from a farm. Her breasts were barely hidden beneath a stained shirt. Her shorts were ripped up. An energy drink tattoo rested above her colossal breasts. Her hair was pulled up as a discolored sweat dripped from her face. The putrid funk of a petting zoo stung my nose.

"London?!" The man shouted at me.

My distressed eyes finally stopped watering long enough for me to recognize him. "Spoons?"

"Come here!" He hoisted me up in his massive arms.

"Put me down! You didn't even wash your hands! Did you just have sex with this girl in there?!"

"Yeah!" Spoons exclaimed, proudly.

"What part of a porta-potty could possibly turn you on? Does this hotbox of feces scream sexual stimulation to you?"

"Yes."

I turned to the girl. "Hi, it's nice to meet you. You're very pretty. I'm sure your parents are proud."

I hoped that she was far too intoxicated to ever remember the terrible decisions she made that day. Then I prayed that I was too intoxicated to remember the terrible decisions she made that day. I let Spoons know.

"Oh, c'mon. You said the same thing last night," Spoons replied.

"You remember what happened last night after Piper left?" I asked.

"Of course. After she left, we hid the machete because we didn't want to die. Then the drag queen performed."

"There was a drag queen last night?"

"Yeah. Don't you remember him getting mad at you?"

I thought about it for a minute before it all clicked and my fuzzy memory came racing back.

There definitely was a drag queen that performed at the party. He got mad at me for taking away everyone's attention. He was supposed to be the only queen there. I tried to explain to him that I wasn't a drag queen, despite wearing a dress.

A drag queen was a character that basked in the spotlight of performance. I was just a terribly uncomfortable guy wearing a dress, trying to get away from his lesbian friend. I wasn't trying to create a new persona. I wasn't trying to lip sync or dance. I was just trying to make a joke out of a dress code. After trying to explain that to the territorial drag queen, he still seemed to resent my existence.

After all the martinis and wine, I was far too intoxicated to drive home. I couldn't even find my car if I had wanted to. I ended up trying to walk the short distance back to my parents' house. Thankfully, I had chosen to wear flats instead of attempting to learn how to move in heels that night.

As I stumbled around the streets at 2 a.m. wearing a little cocktail dress, a group of guys hanging around a park shouted at me. I kept my head down and minded my own business, but that didn't stop them from yelling aggressive compliments. I increased my speed, but the guys were determined to get some sort of reaction from me. They caught up only to be disappointed that I wasn't female.

"You a faggot, man?" One of the guys demanded.

"A little faggot in a dress," another one answered.

I was panicked. I was disoriented. I was outnumbered and defenseless. One of the guys reached for my arm, but I moved away just in time and ran. Despite the tiny dress, I managed to gain enough speed to get away.

Spoons, his lady friend, and I reached the exit of the Pride event, searching for Kristina and Piper. I looked around noticing a lot of guys wearing dresses—some were drag queens, others were just guys that enjoyed wearing dresses.

There were women wearing pants and sports bras; there were shirtless transgender men; there were non-binary people wearing only underwear. People were wearing whatever they felt comfortable in with no judgment.

This was what Pride was really about. It wasn't about getting free stuff from companies that realized the LGBT+ community was a profitable group if they slapped a rainbow on a product. It wasn't about free samples of toothpaste or drinking so much that medical attention was needed.

L.A. Pride was about feeling safe. It was about being able to celebrate who we were among our own community. We may have all been different from each other, but we came together to celebrate that we were all under the queer umbrella.

As I was looking at the colorful but thinning crowd on the boulevard, I heard an obnoxious whistle in the distance.

"Dick whistle!" I pointed.

Piper ran up to us blowing the plastic toy with Kristina behind her. We all headed toward my car where I gave Spoons the unenviable task of driving us home.

I sat in the back with Kristina, Piper, and the bags full of all the free stuff we snagged. Spoons' lady friend kept him company in the front seat. By that point, we were all used to the mysterious stench that radiated from her. Piper was completely knocked out. We finally found solace in the silence of Kristina's bubbly voice. My head leaned on her as I was finding my own unconscious euphoria. Thankfully, the 605 freeway was clear, and we'd be home in no time.

Just as my body was shutting down, ready to produce much needed melatonin, my eyes shot open.

"Um, Spoons?" I said, alarmed.

"Yeah?"

"Can you stop at a restroom?" My voice shook.

"We're almost home. Five more minutes," he assured me.

"I don't think I can wait. Just stop at a restaurant."

"It's the middle of the night—nothing is open."

"Spoons!"

"All right, I'll find a gas station at the next exit."

"Jesus," I said. "Pull over now!"

"On the freeway?"

"NOW!"

Spoons pulled onto the shoulder of the 605 freeway. I leaped out of the car taking two giant steps across the gravel next to a car bumper, half a couch, and other miscellaneous freeway garbage that nobody knew the origins of. I pulled down my jeans that got even tighter from the day's sweat. I squatted, expelling the demons from my body. A mixture of binge drinking, Taco Bell, and dancing created the perfect storm of bowel movements on the side of the freeway. The sweet release felt like a dripping orgasm until I realized I had nothing to wipe with.

I wasn't an animal. I wasn't going to go back into the car without cleaning myself up. I thought about using my socks, but there was no way I could keep my balance while taking one off. The headlights of cars rushing by were illuminating me with embarrassment. I pulled my shirt up over my head and used it to dry up the residue with a few quick wipes. I pulled my pants up and tossed my favorite V-neck as far as I could.

Spoons, his lady friend, and Kristina stared at me, registering what they had just witnessed. Piper forced her eyes open.

"Did that just happen?" Piper asked.

"Yes," Spoons answered. "He just shit on the 605 freeway."

"You mean the Shit-O-Five freeway," Kristina corrected.

They laughed as we sped away. On the side of the freeway, among the other miscellaneous garbage, rested a black V-neck stained with the memories of Jack Daniels, a Cheesy Gordita Crunch, and a lot of pride.

NIGHT OF 1,000 VOMITS

"**F**uck Israel. Do not let him in!"

"Aren't you guys friends?" Spoons asked.

"Yeah. I guess. He's more friends with Tristan than me. I don't want either one of them near my party."

"Still bitter about the breakup? I thought you were the one that broke it off with Tristan?"

"I'm not bitter," I replied. "I just don't want terrible humans at my house. You're the only exception."

"You're being dramatic."

"Just don't let them in."

"Fine," Spoons confirmed as the security guard to my party.

Anytime my parents went away for a weekend, I took the opportunity to throw a raging party that would last the entire three days. My parents would leave me twenty dollars for pizza that I'd toss to the nearest of-age person to get a jug of the cheapest vodka they could find. Then I'd raid my parents' liquor cabinet, stealing the bottles that I didn't think they would miss—coffee liqueur, Sour Apple Schnapps, Triple Sec. This would accumulate into a shrine of the worst possible mixes of alcohol, but none of my mostly-underage party guests seemed to mind.

Since starting college, I joined a club called the Gay-

Straight Alliance that introduced me to more LGBT+ people than I had ever met in my life. I would invite every queer person I knew to my party, and they invited all the queers that they knew. Before the sun even set, there would be dozens upon dozens of people crowding the house while I reveled in the company. None of us had much in common aside from our love of the same sex, partying, and the relief of no longer being in High School.

It was barely 9 p.m. when some people were already passing out while more people came shuffling in. People were welcomed to stay the night or the entire weekend. There were only two rules for entry: everyone had to be intoxicated from either alcohol or drugs, and nobody was allowed to throw up. One of these rules was always broken.

"Didn't you say you were done drinking for the night?" I asked Milo, as he sauntered up to me shoveling a neon orange Jell-O shot into his mouth.

"I am. I'm just eating Jell-O now," he replied.

"You know that... never mind."

Milo was one of my best friends and the first transgender person I had ever met. He was the epitome of a lightweight when it came to alcohol and was clueless as to just how much low-quality vodka was used to make the Jell-O shots. There was no doubt that he would soon find out.

"Where did you disappear to?" Milo asked.

"Just had a talk with Spoons," I answered.

"You told him not to let Israel and Tristan in again, didn't you?"

"Unfortunately, I have to tell that big lug multiple times."

"Why are you trying to exclude people?"

"Because they're garbage," I explained, poorly.

"No, they're not. Tristan might be a little... off. But Israel is sweet. He's just always attached to Tristan," Milo returned.

"A little off? Ha!"

Milo slurped down another Jell-O shot.

"You do know there's alcohol in those, right?" I asked.

"Yeah, but not really enough to get drunk off of."

"Sure."

A high-pitched laughter cut through the air.

"It's them," I declared, marching toward the front door.

"Wait, don't—" But before Milo's orange-stained face could finish, I was already moving toward the cackling.

I rounded the corner to see Israel and Tristan laughing with Spoons. Tristan looked the same as he did the last time I saw him, when we broke up—tired and confused. He previously had an addiction to methamphetamine and currently had a problem with drinking too much. He was the type of person that needed to be the center of attention at any cost. He wanted everyone to feel bad and take care of him, even though he had no desire to take care of himself.

Israel was the opposite. He was caring and nurturing. He also had an overwhelming desire to be needed. With his lack of self-confidence, he got validation by helping people. This was a lethal combination with Tristan's personality. It only made sense that the two of them were inseparable.

The only reason I was still acquainted with them was because we ran in the same social circle of queers and there weren't a lot of options of other people to hang out with. I didn't mind being around them at school, but I didn't want them at my parents' house, and they knew it.

I stood face-to-face with the uninvited guests while Spoons stood to the side.

"Spoons, we just talked about this," I shouted at the pushover.

"I can't just reject them," Spoons shrugged.

"Yeah, we're coming in," Tristan announced. "Your parties suck without us, anyway. Everybody came for us."

"Don't get mad, girl," Israel said, off of my look. "He's just kidding. You know we love you."

He gave me a hug, smirking as he pulled away.

Milo swayed up to us, passing out Jell-O shots like Halloween candy.

"You guys made it!" He slurred.

"Ew, those aren't vegan," Tristan replied, pushing past the shots toward the party. My eyes darted to Israel who only shrugged.

"Don't be like that," Israel suggested. "You're too dramatic."

"Let's enjoy the night," Spoons added.

"You're aware you're the worst security of all time, right?" I asked.

"Yeah. Cheers!" Spoons held up his shot with Milo, Israel, and myself.

I let the potent gelatin wiggle its way down my throat, making a splash into all the alcohol I had previously consumed. Before I could even regret the decision, a scream emitted from my room.

I raced across the party, cutting through a crowd of people dancing. I yanked open the door to my room. A few people shoved their way out. I searched past them to see one of my friends dry heaving on my bed. She tried to get off but kept falling back. I grabbed the nearest trashcan and leaped over empty alcohol bottles. She reached for her purse. Before I could get to her, she expelled her stomach fluids directly into her bag.

"Why is it so chunky?!" I shouted.

Her stomach dipped and launched once more into her purse. It appeared like this girl never even chewed her food. Her bile was coming out like a can of SpaghettiOs exploding into her bag. Part of me was glad that she didn't puke on my floor, but another part of me was bummed that she was sitting on my bed.

Tristan stood in the corner giggling and taking pictures of the girl. He chugged his beer between clicks of his phone. I helped her out of my room, carrying her purse that looked like a sinking ship. She must not have had tampons in it because nothing was being absorbed.

After getting her outside, I examined my bed for remnants of food. I stripped the sheets and carried them through the dozens of people dancing outside. They quickly parted. The stench of digested food rose toward my face. I raced to the laundry room as quickly as I could. I hurried through the door, finding a hefty woman sprawled across the washer and dryer.

"Excuse me, can you stop masturbating on my parents' appliances please?" I asked.

"Oh, I wasn't. I was—"

I waved my hand indicating that I didn't need—nor want —an explanation. The girl buttoned her pants then slid off the washer. An indentation remained from her impressive posterior.

"You must have came here with Spoons," I said without question, as I shoved the stained sheets into the crying washing machine.

"How did you know?" The masturbator asked.

"You seem like a Spoons girl. It's a pleasure to meet you."

Spoons clearly had a type, and the only people that didn't know it were the new girls he brought to each occasion. They all looked identical so much that I wouldn't have had a clue if I met them before or not. They were all curvy white girls that lacked rhythm and ass but made up for with colossal breasts. The girls were typically threes on the hotness scale and sevens on the Richter (not that there was anything wrong with that). Usually, they had drool stains on their shirts which ensured that they were STD-free because nobody in their right mind would be inside them without securely wrapping themselves. Of course, these girls had the sweetest and most fun personalities because—let's be honest—they had to.

I headed back outside leaving the Spoons girl alone with a now vibrating washer. The backyard was filling with more and more people. A lot of them I knew—most of them I didn't.

A puff of smoke passed by me. I glanced over to see Israel sitting in the corner by himself, watching the rest of the party dance and socialize.

"Come over here. Sit down," he invited me, patting the chair beside him.

"Why are you by yourself in the corner?" I asked.

"There's a lot of people here."

"Definitely more than I expected."

"Is that why you look so worried?" He asked. "You don't look like you're having fun."

"I don't know..." I trailed off.

"Is it Tristan? He's changed, girl. He's a much better person now."

"Didn't he OD at the bathhouse last week?"

"He said someone drugged him," Israel said.

"And you believe that?"

"Of course. He's my best friend and I'm his only friend."

"I wonder why," I scoffed. "Remember that time he disappeared on your birthday and came back with a bloody face? He told us he got jumped, only for us to find out he just fell into a bush?"

"He said he got drugged that night too."

"Choosing to smoke meth isn't getting drugged!" I shouted, a little too loud.

"Just trust me. He's changed. He's had a rough life."

"Maybe you're right."

I took a deep breath and decided to actually enjoy my party. I wandered toward the beer pong area and took a few "celebrity" shots. It was always fun to see my parents find ping-pong balls in the bushes weeks after the parties. They wondered why we loved playing ping-pong so much and why we always lost the balls.

After chugging a few beers, I made my way to an impressive stoner circle that took up nearly the entire perimeter of the backyard. Multiple blunts were going around as well as a bong. I took my first bong rip. My lungs ached with an uncontrollable cough that followed. Once I was able to breathe again, I made my way toward the stereo system.

A crowd of people had been dancing nonstop for the last few hours. Their pupils were huge and sweat rolled down their bodies despite their lack of clothing. The ecstasy was in abundance that night as three CDs kept playing on a loop. We were all too poor to afford an iPod but always had enough money for drugs. Like the people on ecstasy, the party was at one of its many peaks that it would hit throughout the weekend.

I sauntered toward the restroom to finally break my seal. When I opened the door, I was blinded by the biggest, whitest breasts I had ever seen in my entire life. They bounced off the sink like two overly inflated basketballs on a court, as Spoons was thrusting behind them. He didn't stop despite me standing in the doorway. He giggled and the girl that dented my parents' washing machine moaned louder.

"Every time I open a damn door, you're fucking someone," I said to Spoons with malice and a hint of pride. I slammed the door shut to give the romantic couple some privacy. I accepted that I would have to burn down the restroom to disinfect it or call an exorcist.

I happily returned to the backyard in search of a nice corner to relieve myself in. Drake played over the stereo, serenading my flow. A couple of people stood next to me following suit, since Spoons had officially marked the restroom as his territory and nobody was going to fight him for it. As the strangers and I bonded over the newly designated pissing area, Tristan bolted out of my room, screaming.

"I didn't do it! I didn't do it!"

More yelling erupted from inside my room followed by a guy running out with tears streaming his face. His boyfriend caught up to him. When they came face-to-face, the crying guy pulled his hand back and launched it with a stiff slap to his boyfriend's face.

"What the hell did you do?!" I yelled at Tristan.

"I didn't do it!" He repeated.

"He didn't do anything," Israel defended him from the corner.

Tristan started toward the crying guy that was ready to square up for a fight. The commotion was enough for Spoons to tear himself away from his lady friend. He interjected, doing the first useful thing he had done all night. He diverted Tristan away from the couple. The couple went into another room while Tristan was being detained in mine like a holding cell.

Israel remained sitting in the corner, lighting up a new cigarette.

"Uh-oh," Spoons said, just as I was about to get to the bottom of whatever had just happened.

Spoons keeled over into my mom's vegetable garden, releasing a torrent of vomit. He crumbled to his knees, soaking the ripe tomatoes. On all fours, he continued spewing bile, christening the produce. Everyone scattered trying to suppress their own gagging.

Tristan was trying to break the door down to get out of my room. The sun was rising as the party descended into chaos.

"What happened?!" I interrogated Tristan.

"I sucked his dick," he replied, casually.

"Wasn't he passed out with his boyfriend?"

"Yeah. So? He still got hard," Tristan said, proudly.

"He's just drunk," Israel said, standing up for his friend. "He probably didn't eat anything earlier."

"Tristan, you can't just suck a stranger's dick!" I informed him.

"Why not?"

"I mean, you can. Just not when they're passed out with their boyfriend," I answered.

"But, like, he was hard."

"You can't just—Why do I have to explain consent to you?!" I shouted.

"I don't care. He liked it and I'll do it again!"

Tristan shoved past Israel and me, running toward the room holding the couple. I dashed after him. Before Tristan could put his hand on the doorknob, I lunged forward, tackling him into the wall.

My head bounced against a corner as I forcefully restrained him from sucking a penis. I locked my arms under his in an anti-cock-sucking Full Nelson and we both crashed onto the ground.

"Stop trying to suck his dick!" I yelled.

"Never!"

The door swung open. The crying guy darted out pulling his boyfriend with him. They went straight to the front door, leaving the madhouse. Tristan and I tried to catch our breaths while still interlocked on the floor. Israel strutted over, laughing.

"I need another drink," Tristan slurred.

"I'll get you one," Israel told him.

I jumped up. "This is exactly why I didn't want you guys here! Tristan is toxic to everyone and all you do is enable him!"

"He's my best friend," Israel shrugged.

"If you're going to keep hanging around him, then I don't want you around me."

"He just drank a little too much. Someone must have given him liquor instead of beer."

"You guys need to leave. Now."

Israel stared at me, realizing how serious I was. He reluctantly forced Tristan to leave with him. The sun had fully risen. Most people had left and would be back sometime in the afternoon.

Miraculously, Spoons returned to making out with the same girl. I didn't know who I felt worse for considering Spoons spent a good portion of the night puking.

The remaining few people were passed out in awkward positions. One of them was Milo. He sat upright in a chair next to the dwindling alcohol shrine. He slowly regained consciousness when I approached.

"Did everyone leave already?" He asked, oblivious to anything that had transpired.

I poured myself a shot of the only thing that was left. The thick, syrupy liquid of Sour Apple Schnapps dribbled from the bottle into a glass. As Milo watched, his eyes glazed over. The color in his cheeks disappeared. Then, a single bomb of projectile vomit launched at the ground, splashing like a water balloon. Losing the battle with gravity, he crashed face first into his puke and laid motionless on the floor.

"Milo, are you okay?" I ran over. "Here, let me help you."

"No, I'm good," he answered. "Just leave me."

Despite him looking rather comfortable in a pool of brown regurgitation that was once neon gelatin, I dragged him back to the chair.

I returned to the shot I poured myself. I held it in the air, surveying the carnage of the party around me. I downed the green apple-flavored booze and slammed the glass down. Immediately, my cheeks filled with regret.

HOLLYWOOD

Years went by after the Night of a Thousand Vomits. All my friends that were at that party drifted apart, branching off into their own little groups within the LGBT+ community. The lesbians dedicated their lives to whoever they were dating at the time; the flamboyant boys were on endless benders; the introverts were content smoking pot and watching Netflix. It seemed as though everyone was finding their niche within the queer community except me.

I wasn't sure where I belonged or if there was even a place I would feel welcomed. I felt like no matter what part of the LGBT+ community I explored, I had to compromise who I was in order to fit in. I tried to like Madonna and Lana Del Rey, but I didn't really connect with that kind of music. Disneyland was pretty cool but not enough to get an annual pass. I didn't frequent the gym enough to make fitness a lifestyle. I wasn't on the "DL", but I also wasn't parading glitter.

I shed my phase of wearing makeup, bright colors, and outrageous hairdos. I returned to my original style, before I was introduced to the gay world. I wore black clothes, Doc

Martens, and a messy hairstyle. I covered myself in more tattoos and piercings. I continued listening to bands like She Wants Revenge, The Germs, and Marilyn Manson. I was unapologetically open about my sexuality, but that wasn't enough to magnetize anyone with the same interests.

There was nothing convincing me to stay in my hometown any longer. I packed up a few essentials and moved thirty miles west into the heart of Hollywood.

*　　　*　　　*

I was the only one of my friends that moved out of their parents' house. I felt like a king living in my own place. If I wanted to walk around naked, I could. If I wanted to leave out lines of cocaine, I could. I was the rule maker of my seven-foot by seven-foot bachelor apartment. Sure, I didn't have a kitchen or Wi-Fi, and my bed may have been a broken futon, but at least I was on my own. Besides, a thousand dollars a month for rent was a steal in Hollywood.

I shot up from my futon to the booming sound of my alarm going off. I noticed it had been set for an hour prior which meant I had been completely asleep as it raged. I didn't have time to be impressed by my unconsciousness. I was late for work.

I bumped into a body as I tried to maneuver my way off the slab of material that was smaller than a twin-sized bed. I couldn't recognize the lifeless person with their face buried beneath the pillow. I couldn't remember who I fell asleep next to, but I wasn't startled. It was a common occurrence since living on my own. Like a surprise slumber party that I threw for myself.

I tried to move the blanket to see who it was. Was it the white-trash guy missing a front tooth? Was it the hot but painfully dumb Armenian guy that thought an olive was a type of fish? The world would never know because I didn't want to ask a question that I didn't actually want an answer to. I stopped nudging the body for fear of him wanting to get breakfast together or—worse—talk.

I rolled off the futon remembering how late I was. I bolted out of the apartment, hoping the guy in my bed was just asleep and not dead. My fingers were crossed.

My apartment was near Amoeba Music, so I had to walk quickly up to Hollywood Boulevard. No matter how late I may have been, there was still no chance of me trying to figure out how to run while hungover. I briskly strutted over the Walk of Fame stars of Fleetwood Mac and Jack White on the boulevard.

Normally, I would have just called out of work, but I had already missed two days that week. It was the end of the month and I was far from having enough rent. Although I was making impressive money bartending at a poolside hotel bar, I was spending it even faster.

I felt the whiskey sweat out of my body as I approached an intersection. I was already an hour and a half late when I noticed a very alluring Starbucks. What would an extra five minutes be? I was going to get reprimanded regardless of how late I was, might as well have had some caffeine in the process. I waited in the Starbucks line that took much longer than five minutes. I treated myself to a well-deserved coffee.

I continued along the boulevard passing all the homeless people, the street performers, Scientologists, and Mr. Muscles —the pot-bellied man that wandered around, aggressively flexing his biceps at people. I darted through a sea of tourists that not only had zero sense of urgency, but crowded around the stars on the floor, making a nearly impossible human barrier for anyone that had to go by. I couldn't possibly care less that I was getting in the way of family photographs of Shrek's star on the ground.

As I was pushing my way through, I bumped into a shaggy individual. I nearly spilled my coffee on Chewbacca— or at least a person dressed as him. Random people dressing up in disgusting, poorly-made character costumes was just as much a staple of Hollywood Boulevard as the Walk of Fame. I had met the acquaintances of such icons as homeless Mickie Mouse, Asian Minnie Mouse, and abuela Batman. However, this was my first encounter with a wooky. He let out his trademark growl as we stood at the final intersection before the mall on Hollywood and Highland.

"Good morning, Chewy," I replied, still a bit tipsy.

Chewy and I raced across the street to our respective jobs. He met up with Freddy Krueger and Wonder Woman while I took the elevator to the top floor of the mall where the hotel's pool bar was located.

I strolled through the glass door entrance to the pool area then into the bar. A gang of tourists and a few reality show "celebrities" were already poolside when I started preparing the bar.

After getting ice, putting down bar mats, and turning on the radio, I exerted all the energy I had for that day, including anything in reserve. I downed the rest of my coffee and started pouring myself a hefty cup of Jameson to ease the hangover before making myself visible to the public.

"What are you doing?" My manager rounded the corner, startling me.

I dropped the Jameson bottle back into its spot with an echoing clank, knowing full well that being caught drinking on the job would lead to immediate termination.

"Nothing," I replied.

"You're late again?" He interrogated.

"It's not my fault. My alarm didn't go off and—"

"You went out drinking again last night, didn't you?"

"No."

The smell of the Irish whiskey in my cup rose to my face, simultaneously making me gag and telling me that I just needed one sip to ease the devil kicking around inside my head.

"I'm going to have to write you up if you're late again," my manager lectured. "And you already have too many write-ups. The next step would be termination."

"C'mon, man."

"It's not my policy. I don't want to do it. But, you know how the hotel is. You got to play by their rules."

I was relieved when he finally turned around so I could get back to my alcohol cure.

"Oh," he said, turning back to me. He pointed at my ears.

"You can't be wearing gauges here anymore."

I reluctantly removed my piercings. The hotel was getting more and more conservative with new rules every week, despite being in liberal Hollywood. I didn't understand the rule about the gauges, considering I had a full tattoo sleeve and a new tattoo on my face.

I finally took a gulp of whiskey then turned back to setting up the bar.

"Hey, did you log in the inventory count yesterday?" My manager interrupted again.

"I'll put in the numbers today," I promised.

For some reason completely lost on me, he thought it was a good idea to let a twenty-two-year-old bartender be responsible for keeping track of all the bottles of liquor. I was in charge of making sure they were all accounted for. What this really meant was that, once a week, I would steal a couple bottles of liquor without removing them from the inventory sheet. The bar wouldn't lose any alcohol—at least not on paper —and I had an endless supply of free booze.

The rest of the day was pretty routine. The array of characters that graced the pool made it feel like I was working in a zoo full of Hollywood's most exotic creatures. There were sloppy Dance Moms that held their children to high standards but didn't care about their own appearance, rich Middle Eastern kids whose parents were royalty in their home countries strutted around like they owned the place, and—my personal favorite—the drunk Clown Lady.

The pool was reserved for people that were staying at the hotel only. However, strangers from the boulevard found their way up to the rooftop all the time. The protocol was to call security on anyone that looked like they didn't belong. The Clown Lady was one of those people.

The Clown Lady spent her mornings on the boulevard making balloon animals for tourists. After putting in her hours of "work", she would find her way up to the pool area still in full clown makeup and an outfit that looked like Raggedy Ann on heroin. My manager informed me that I needed to call security to kick her out anytime I saw her. Of course, I never did that because the Clown Lady was my favorite human in Hollywood. Instead, I would feed her free drinks to encourage her erratic behavior simply because she made me feel better about my own life.

That day, the Clown Lady brought two special guests to the pool with her. The first was her pimp. The second was her fourteen-year-old daughter. I wasn't sure if I was surprised by either.

"How much are fucking quesadillas?!" The Clown Lady shouted in shock. "Jesus wouldn't charge that much! You're fucking robbing me, man."

"It's not my choice," I shrugged. "So you just want a drink then?"

"Hell no, give me that quesadilla. That shit is so good. And the drink too."

"The drink is on the house, but I do I have to charge you for the food."

"That's fine," she slurred. "Hang on a second." She swayed back over to a tall, old black man that pulled a wad of hundred-dollar bills from his pocket. He handed her one, and she returned to pay for her food.

After devouring her grossly overpriced quesadilla, the Clown Lady stripped down to her bathing suit—or maybe it was her bra and panties. Either way, her left nipple hung out the side of her top after jumping into the pool with her daughter. I hoped that the teenage girl wasn't too damaged by her mother's decisions in life. The Clown Lady was setting a bad example by willingly paying sixteen dollars for a quesadilla.

Despite the entertainment of watching peoples' lives, I was ecstatic for my shift to finally be over. I plugged in the inventory numbers after I decided which bottle of booze I was going to steal. I shoved the expensive Johnny Walker Gold Label into my backpack along with Red Bulls, a couple of beers, an oversized Rice Krispie Treat, and an orange (because I couldn't be completely unhealthy).

"You done?" My manager asked.

"What?" I stammered, zipping up my backpack.

"You done for the day?"

"Yeah. All finished. See you tomorrow."

"On time. Don't make me be the bad guy," he warned.

I raced home much faster than I had raced to work. The bottles of alcohol clinked in my backpack as I passed Chewbacca and friends. I got to my apartment, relieved to find that whichever guy was in my bed that morning had already left. Which also meant that he was alive and that was a good thing too. I changed my clothes, grabbed my car, and drove to WeHo because, after a rough hungover day, I deserved a drink.

"Hey, you fuck face. What brings you 'round?" Grayson spat from behind the bar with warm hospitality.

"I came to see you, princess," I said to the dive bar owner.

"Piss off." He punched me in the ribs. "What'ya havin'?"

"Let's do the usual, but I got to take it slow. I'm driving today."

One of my biggest fears was getting a DUI. I could put up with having my driver's license suspended, paying thousands of dollars in fines, and the overall shame of being placed in a holding cell. However, I could not fathom mandatory A.A. meetings.

Grayson lined up two shots for us.

"As we say in England, 'down the hatch'. As we say in WeHo, 'bottoms up'." We knocked our glasses together and downed the liquor.

As the afternoon progressed, I learned a valuable lesson: you can't out-drink an Englishman, especially when he was twice my age.

The only dive bar in WeHo was having a typical afternoon. Lost tourists wandered inside with their families, homeless people begged for free drinks, closeted gay men pretended they didn't know it was a gay area despite the rainbow-painted crosswalk outside.

Two conventionally attractive guys sat in the far corner of the bar. They were traditional WeHo-looking guys—thin, white, blond. One of them was tall like a model. The other one was tiny like a sugar daddy's dream boy. I couldn't help but stare as they engaged in a heated argument.

"They're in here all the time," Grayson informed me. "Both a bit mad. The tall one is Aiden and his boyfriend is James."

"They're kind of cute," I said, closing one eye to focus.

"No," Grayson said, flatly.

"Well, they're the cutest ones here."

"You're a wanker," he said, realizing that we were the only other people in the bar.

A shouting match between Aiden and James escalated. I tried to mind my own business, but the bar was so tiny that it was impossible not to hear the arguing. Finally, Aiden stormed out of the bar leaving his boyfriend.

"Aw, poor guy," I whispered to Grayson.

"Ha! Don't act like you feel bad for 'em," he scoffed.

"How could I not? He's crying in the corner by himself."

I got up from my barstool and crossed over to James.

"You okay?" I asked.

"Fine," James replied, wiping his tears.

"You can come sit with me if you want."

"Thanks, but I have to figure out how I'm getting home. He took the car."

"Oh. I can drive you if you want."

He shot me a look.

"I'm not trying to hit on you," I lied. "I'll just drop you off and come back here."

I wasn't sure if I was making a bad decision by offering to drive, or if James was making a worse decision by accepting.

I staggered with the cute guy to the alley behind the bar where my car was parked. I could barely keep my feet steady as I pulled out my keys. I struggled to put the key in the lock, leaving scratches all over the handle. Ego was dominating my better judgment. I looked like a savior coming to the rescue of the poor guy that was ditched at the bar by his boyfriend. I finally got the car unlocked when Aiden rounded the corner.

"What are you doing with my boyfriend?" The tall guy yelled.

"Just giving him a ride home. No intentions of anything

else," I said, not even convincing myself.

"You're the one who left me," James interjected. "He was just giving me a ride."

Aiden took a long stride toward me with his lanky body. James cut him off with his tiny figure. I couldn't help but laugh at the size difference. It was an odd sight to see someone so tall be restrained by someone a foot shorter. Before I could laugh anymore, Aiden's long arm reached over his boyfriend. His fist came flying at my face, connecting with my right eye.

My adrenaline spiked. My fists came up. It was only the third time I had ever been punched. Despite deserving it, I was ready to trade blows.

I leaned in on the offensive before Aiden could catch me off-guard again. James kept himself between us. Before I could get any closer, James reached up shoving his boyfriend against a car. He pulled his arm back and released a cavalcade of infant-sized punches into his boyfriend's face. Aiden's eyes welled with tears.

"What the actual fuck," I whispered to myself.

That level of relationship dysfunction was far beyond my comprehension capacity. I slipped away from the alley, knowing I couldn't possibly do any more damage than they were already doing to themselves. My adrenaline subsided, allowing me to feel the pounding of my swelling face. My head started spinning. The warmth of saliva gathered in my mouth. I stumbled back to the bar as quickly as I could. I ran into the restroom, wasting all the alcohol I had consumed. I returned to the barstool.

"Grayson, I didn't even get a punch in! How am I going to let someone hit me and not do anything about it?!" I shouted.

"Just leave it alone. There's no point in getting into a scuffle. Especially here."

Grayson and I were friends even outside of the bar, but his response felt more from the perspective of a business owner that didn't want to be liable rather than from a friend. I couldn't help but believe if we were out drinking somewhere else, he would have encouraged a fight.

My drunk ego was weighing me down. I couldn't shake the thought that I didn't even properly defend myself. I slipped out of the bar again when Grayson wasn't looking. I made my way back to the alley, hoping that Aiden was still lingering.

I stood in the tiny alley alone. The only things around me were dumpsters and parked cars. I contemplated just driving home, feeling like I had seen enough action that day, but I was still far too intoxicated to unlock my car door. I sighed turning around.

"Looking for me?" Aiden asked, emerging from the shadows.

I threw my fists up.

"Why were you trying to steal my boyfriend?" He asked. "Why would you do that? Where were you going? Why..."

I couldn't process anything he was saying. Everything came out muffled. The only thing I could focus on was a receipt for getting punched in the face. I lunged toward him. He took a step back with his hands down to his side. He had no intention of fighting, but I had other plans. Every time I stepped forward, he stepped back and continued talking.

I was getting frustrated. My testosterone needed some kind of release. Then, warm saliva gathered in my mouth. I could feel straggling chunks of vomit crawling back up my throat. I cocked my head back and launched a vomit-filled glob of spit directly into Aiden's eye, hoping it would entice him to fight.

He stood with his face coated with my stomach fluids. He was stunned trying to wipe it off. I was in a bit of shock myself that I did that. But my plan failed. Aiden turned around refusing to engage. He sauntered away disappearing into the alley.

I strutted back to the bar only semi-satisfied.

"But I didn't get a punch in!" I whined to Grayson again, as I helped him close down the bar for the night.

"Sure, but you spit in his face, didn't ya? How humiliating is that?"

That wasn't enough to please my bruised ego, but it would have to suffice.

Despite my fear of a DUI, I felt sober enough to drive the two miles home. I hopped into my car, finally able to get my door unlocked with minimal effort. I pulled up to the first intersection, acknowledging just how blurry everything was. I drove past a police station as casually as I could. It was a straight shot home from there.

As I cruised along Santa Monica Boulevard, mindful of the speed limit, I saw my car get dangerously close to the car in the lane to the right of me. I jerked the steering wheel the opposite direction, nearly landing in oncoming traffic. My heart raced. My knuckles turned white gripping the wheel. Maybe I hadn't sobered up as much as I thought I had.

I looked over to the car I almost hit—again it was dangerously close. But this time, I knew I wasn't the one swerving. The car raced up, becoming parallel to mine. Through the window, I saw Aiden raise his hand in a facetious wave as he drove. He smiled at me before turning his wheel toward my car, trying to run me into the opposite lane. I sped up to avoid the impact. The maniac landed behind me.

"Holy balls!" I yelled.

Aiden gained speed along my car, brushing against it. I could see him through the mirror, laughing. I debated going down a side street to get away, but I couldn't slow my car down long enough to make a turn. Aiden bumped my car again. I gripped the wheel tight, trying to prevent the wheels from locking up.

Out of nowhere, a giant, white truck pulled in front of Aiden's car. Aiden slammed down onto his brakes forcing his car to skid to a stop. I looked into my side mirror to see the window of the truck roll down.

"Really, Aiden? Do you really want to do this?!" The fiery Englishman spat.

I took the opportunity to quickly turn onto a side street. I zigzagged through a residential area to avoid anybody following me. Miraculously, I reached my apartment without any psychotic homos or police sirens chasing after me. I ran up to my room, threw off my sweaty clothes, and took a much-needed shower to calm my nerves.

When I got out, I was finally able to relax. I laid in bed scrolling through social media when I came across a message on Facebook from Aiden:

Sorry about tonight. Drank a little too much.

"No shit," I said to myself. I was wary about his message being some sort of trap that he wanted me to engage in. I couldn't see how it could be, though. Besides, I was a bit of an asshole for swooping in on his boyfriend. I took the high road:

Sorry I spit in your face.

He responded:

It's okay. I kinda liked when you spit in my face.

The next thing I knew, Aiden's face was buried into a pillow as he screamed and moaned with pleasure. I may have never thrown the punch that I wanted to throw, but the violent sex with him made up for it. Because, let's face it, I kind of liked when I spit in his face too.

I woke up on the floor of a West Hollywood luxury apartment. Next to me was a naked person facedown on a pillow. I noticed the red handprints all over his body and, this time, knew exactly who was laying next to me. I crossed my fingers hoping Aiden was still alive, but also hoping that he wouldn't wake up before I snuck out of his apartment.

A muffled sound echoed from across the room. A piercing headache struck me as soon as the noise reached my ears. My hangovers were conditioned to strike as soon as I heard my alarm. I lifted a pile of clothes, shaking the phone out of my pants.

"Shit," I whispered, careful not to wake the sleeping psychopath.

I had barely enough time to make it to work without being late. I threw on my clothes and rushed out of the apartment.

As with any building I passed out in, I didn't have a clue which direction to go. I took the first available turn down a long hallway. I made another sharp left, passing a mother taking her child to school. I hit a dead end forcing me to retrace the labyrinth in another direction.

I could feel dried body fluids against my skin. I was in desperate need of a shower but didn't have time. I turned another corner finally finding the elevator. Of course, it was one of the elevators that had a star next to level four, leaving me to wonder what the first three floors were and where my car was. I took a chance pressing a number.

Thankfully, it led me to the parking lot. I pressed my key remote incessantly until my car beeped. I slid in, peeled out of the parking spot, and drove up to the garage door. It didn't move. I pulled up closer. Still nothing. I nearly touched the gate with my bumper. I couldn't think of a worse time to find out the garage door was not automatic. I had to choose between navigating the maze back into the building to get Aiden to let me out or leave my car and run to work. I chose the latter.

I ran all the way to work. I passed multiple coffee shops but decided against stopping. I couldn't risk getting fired. I raced over the stars of Steve Harvey and Madonna. I stopped at an intersection waiting for the light.

"Gwarrhww!" a familiar growl bellowed next to me.

"Not now, Chewy," I told Chewbacca.

I darted across the street to Hollywood and Highland. I sprinted up five flights of stairs because it would have taken longer shoving my way through tourists to get to the elevator. I reached the top floor, entering the glass doors to the pool bar. I took my gauges out. I poured myself a cup of water and chugged it. I struggled to catch my breath.

"You went out drinking again, didn't you?" My manager asked me.

"No. Definitely not," I choked.

"Well, at least you made it on time," he laughed. "You put the inventory in?"

"Yesterday."

"Good," he said, turning toward his desk.

That must have been what it felt like to be an adult. I had actually put in an effort to make it to work on time. I recognized there would be consequences to being late, so I avoided them. I learned my lesson from the last time. I felt like I was growing up and finally becoming responsible.

"Oh, by the way, you need to start covering your tattoos, otherwise we can't have you working here anymore. The hotel wants us to be more conservative."

I looked at my tattoo sleeve then at the tattoos on my legs. I could feel my new face tattoo healing. I calmly finished my cup of water. I left the bar and marched toward the pool. Hotel guests lounged on the surrounding chairs. The pool was completely still. The Hollywood sign reflected off the surface. I pulled my shirt off, tossing it aside. My Doc Martens stomped over the gleaming hotel floor. I gained speed sprinting toward the pool. I launched myself into the air, diving into the icy water. The faint sound of gasps disappeared as I submerged. The water engulfed me. The wetness soothed my sun-kissed skin; the cold hydrated my hungover body; the silence expelled all my thoughts, even for just a moment.

I wasn't sure why I had just done that. Maybe it was my inability to conform; maybe it was a decision fueled by my frustration with my life. I didn't think about how I was going to lose my job. I didn't think about the rent that I didn't have. My life was spiraling out of control, driven by an unlimited amount of alcohol and bad choices.

I resurfaced to the stunned faces of the pool guests. One of the maids stared at me in horror as I pulled my soaking body out of the pool. My shorts and boots were weighing me down. I trailed water all the way to the glass doors. I exited without looking back. I took the elevator down to the street. I dripped all the way home on Hollywood Boulevard passed Chewbacca and Wonder Woman, across the stars of Britney Spears and Marilyn Monroe, and into my tiny apartment that I could no longer afford. Then I got the text message:

Did we use a condom last night? You might want to get tested.

PART II

ISADORA

I sat in the LGBT Center waiting room anxious for my name to be called. My eyes were fixated on the neutral-colored carpet that connected to the neutral-colored walls. The inspirational posters that reminded people not to engage in rape hung throughout the room. Everything about that place made me uncomfortable.

My eyes drifted toward the television protruding from the wall. Ariel was combing her hair with a fork in hopes of seducing a human to feed her fishy needs. Her wingman crab friend encouraged. Before that movie started playing, I caught the end of Cinderella who got her happily-ever-after.

There was something about Disney magic that warmed the hearts of the LGBT+ community. Maybe it was being able to watch characters get the happily-ever-after that people in our community never got to experience. Maybe it was the desire to be royalty. Maybe it was the relatable villain that every movie provided. I found myself getting lost in the films. The LGBT Center really knew how to make a queer feel comfortable.

My name was called, snapping me out of my fixation on a

fantasy world. I was escorted to a room full of needles and vials of blood. Four nurses were doing the honors—three female (one lesbian) and an incredibly attractive guy (clearly gay). Usually I would have been happy to be assisted by the tantalizing homo but, because I was already uncomfortable and nervous, I had my fingers crossed for the nice lesbo.

Of course, my life was not a Disney fairytale. None of my wishes were being granted. I was placed in the seat of the male nurse. Adding to my discomfort and overall desire to not be in that room, my hormones were triggered. I tried to not stare at the nurse, but just his presence was enough to get my heart beating rapidly. I tried to stay still as he pierced my arm.

The pheromones were unavoidable. My heart pounded. The vial in my arm was quickly filling up with blood. I was terrified the tube was going to burst. That would have been a ridiculous scenario, though. There was no way there was enough blood in my arm because most of it was flowing down into my genitals.

Thankfully, the whole situation was over within a minute. I was beginning to feel like I was in a strange porn. I hoped that I didn't develop some sort of fetish for guys removing blood from my body. I prayed that next time, the lesbian would be the one sticking sharp objects into me.

Once he removed the needle, I jumped out of my seat before collecting myself. A rush of dizziness swept through my head. I probably should have eaten before getting blood drawn, but it was far too late. I left the Center as quickly as my body would let me. I was already obsessing over receiving my results, even though I was at least a week away before getting them.

I distracted myself by mindlessly scrolling through Facebook, when I got a message from Israel:

Hey girl, I'm back in L.A.

It had been three years since I had seen Israel. The last I had heard, through the grapevine of the few friends we had in common, was that he had moved to San Francisco.

We were making small talk when he asked me where I was

living. I told him I lived on June Street in Hollywood—which wasn't a lie. However, I omitted that I was living in my car and that happened to be the only street in the area that had parking. I had lost my apartment shortly after I quit my job via diving into the pool. Right after, I learned just how difficult it was to find another job in Los Angeles.

Israel messaged me again:

We should hang out.

A lot of time had passed since we last hung out, but I still had no desire to be friends again. I was at capacity of people in my life that I pretended to care about; I had no extra energy. So I did what everyone does as an adult—I told him I would love to hang out "sometime". Which was the universal adult language for 'probably not, but I don't want to be rude'.

I was feeling faint after getting my blood drawn. I had to get some food quick, so I went to the place that kept me fed since becoming unemployed. Every meal of my day was a Subway sandwich for the past few weeks. I'd buy a footlong in the morning and eat half of it. Then for lunch, I'd finish the other half that would be only moderately soggy. For dinner, I would get the daily six-inch special (except Wednesdays because I would have rather starved than eaten tuna). This was the best routine for me to conserve money, fill my body with some substance, and be slightly healthier than other fast-food chains.

I lumbered over to the Subway counter where the employee already had my order memorized. I felt like a fancy suburban mom entering a Starbucks after using an app to order ahead. Except I was at a food chain that had a formerly obese, current child predator as their spokesman.

I slid over to pay for the bland food. I put my credit card into the machine. DECLINED. I tried it again just in case there was an error. DECLINED. Then I tried it once more because I was getting embarrassed and didn't know what else to do. DECLINED. Then I tried a fourth time in hopes that money would magically appear in my bank account.

AGGRESSIVELY DECLINED.

I didn't have enough money to purchase a meager, five-dollar sandwich from Subway. My credit card was maxed out. I was hungry and desperate. I counted some loose change in my pocket, but it was not nearly enough. I went to my car to search for more. Thankfully, I found some spare change scattered throughout. I returned to my sandwich and the annoyed Subway employee. He watched as I counted out my total in coins. I was a few cents short, but he took pity on me with a nickel discount.

I sauntered back to my car on June Street. I sat in the backseat and solemnly ate my dinner. I was defeated and alone. Nobody knew the situation I was in; I was too embarrassed to ask anyone for help. I hadn't told my family or my friends. When I first moved to Los Angeles, I thought I knew what I was getting into. I refused to admit that I was wrong, and that I was making terrible decisions. My foolish pride kept me from seeking the help I desperately needed.

I didn't want to be alone that night, stewing in my own thoughts. I didn't want to talk to anyone, but I would have reveled in the comfort of seeing a familiar face. There was only a handful of people that I knew in L.A. Then I remembered Israel's message.

I messaged him back:

You free tonight?

"Israel, this place is like a mansion!" I exclaimed, exploring his two-bedroom apartment at the peak of a hill in Silver Lake. It was significantly more spacious than my previous bachelor apartment and even more spacious than my car.

"Meh," he answered, humbly.

I took advantage of the luxury of an air conditioner before I explored the kitchen. I couldn't remember the last time I had sat at a dining table or the last time I used an actual plate. I made my way to the refrigerator. The giant rectangle flooded me with jealousy. I put my hand on the door feeling nostalgia over the sound of it opening. Inside, there were three large pizza boxes stacked on the top shelf. I could hear the hymn of angels as I stared at the Holy Grail of food.

"That's a lot of pizza," I said, salivating.

"Eat as much as you want," Israel encouraged. "My work gives them to me for free."

My eyes lit up. I didn't want to seem like a hungry animal, but I was borderline. I pulled a large meat-lover's pizza out and devoured the cold meal. I kept eating even after I was full. My stomach was thrilled to have something other than a sandwich. While I basked in the gluttony, Israel told me about everything he had been doing in San Francisco.

"Yeah, girl, I needed to get away from this place to really find myself. I graduated school and got my life together. I wouldn't have been able to do that hanging around the people here."

I was only paying attention to every few words he was saying. There was too much pepperoni and sausage for me to focus on anything else.

"You're the first person I messaged since being back," Israel continued.

"Really?" I asked, surprised. "What about Tristan?"

"I haven't hit him up yet. I don't really know if I want to."

"What? Why not? You guys are like B-F-Fs."

"I don't know," Israel said. "Things are different now. I'm not the same person I used to be."

I laughed unintentionally.

"You don't believe me?" He asked, offended.

"I don't know," I tried to backtrack. I didn't want to offend the person that was feeding me and letting me loiter on their couch, but I couldn't lie. "You weren't the best person to hang out with, Israel. The only person you ever cared about was Tristan. You put him before everyone else—even before yourself. Not to mention, you were kindle to drama and loved getting into everyone else's business."

"Are you serious?" Israel asked. "Is that how people saw me?"

I froze with a slice of pizza in my mouth. I slowly nodded my head.

"I had no idea people thought of me like that."

I couldn't tell if Israel was genuinely surprised, or if he was feeling guilty. Maybe a combination of both.

"The only time you were fun to be around," I continued, "was when we would go watch drag shows together."

"That's what I've been wanting to tell you," he replied. "I've been doing drag in San Francisco."

"What?" I put the pizza down.

"Yeah. I've been doing shows up there and I've already booked a couple down here."

"You? Doing drag?" I asked. "Why would you want to do drag?"

I didn't know a lot about drag queens. I didn't understand why anyone would want to wear a dress and pretend to sing to a song—especially Israel. He was the kind of person that sat quietly in corners and observed people. He was never the one in the spotlight. He wasn't even the main character in his own life.

"Drag lets me be myself," he answered.

"That's vague."

"I have a show tomorrow night. Just come watch."

"Maybe," I said, with no intention.

After eating his food, sinking into his couch, and abusing his television all evening, I felt like I was overstaying my welcome. I reluctantly pulled myself away from his comfortable couch.

"I think I'm going to head out," I said.

"Aw, no. Stay. We can have a sleepover," he pleaded.

My pride and exhaustion were in a tug-of-war. I was too proud to keep freeloading, but I also didn't have anywhere else to go. I would have ended up sleeping in my car on his street, anyway.

"I don't know…" I said, mostly to myself.

"C'mon, girl. I haven't seen you in forever. Let's catch up. You haven't even told me what you've been up to."

I took a deep breath before sitting back down. I thought

about the weight of all my recent bad decisions catching up to me. I could feel myself crumbling. The consequences of quitting my job, losing my apartment, maxing out credit cards on Venmo-ing drug dealers. Feeling alone in the unmerciful city of Los Angeles was draining. I didn't know what to do anymore. Israel was showing me a generosity and hospitality that I didn't deserve, but that I desperately needed. My eyes welled up with tears.

"What's going on?" He asked.

"I just haven't had a good place to sleep in a while." I tried to hold myself together, but I couldn't anymore. I broke down telling Israel everything that had been happening in my life.

"Don't be stupid!" He told me. "You can stay here whenever!"

"No, I can't do that," I replied.

"Well, I won't force you. But you're always welcome here."

Israel saw through the facade I was putting up. He knew I was struggling, and that I was too proud to ask for help. He didn't want to embarrass me by showing too much sympathy. He knew the more he offered, the less likely it would be that I would accept.

"Thank you," I said, as he handed me a blanket and pillow. "One day, I'll pay you back."

*   *   *

After a night of adequate sleep, being able to fully extend my legs, and enjoying the comfort of not having a seatbelt buckle jamming into my back, I was ready to greet the morning. Well, the afternoon when I woke up. I was feeling like royalty with my breakfast of pizza and caffeinated soda. Israel and I spent the next few hours lounging around, watching movies before it was time for him to start getting into drag for his performance that night.

He opened up a suitcase and, like a more feminine Mary Poppins, things kept exploding from it. Within seconds, his entire apartment was covered with miscellaneous drag attire.

The restroom floor, sink, and bathtub were crowded with every kind of Dollar Store makeup imaginable. His room held an assortment of colored fabrics that looked like a deflated circus tent. Even the hallway had hairbrushes and wigs strewn around.

"What the hell is all this?" I asked, picking up a roll of Duct tape.

"Those are for my tits," Israel replied, casually putting streaks of white makeup onto his face.

"Do you really need this much stuff? And it's not even 5 o'clock yet. We still have hours before the show."

"You can't rush beauty, girl."

Israel had some sort of nylon stocking on his head to hold his hair back. He wore a shirt from Target and men's basketball shorts. He sat on the floor clutching a tiny compact mirror up to his face. I couldn't even begin to imagine how that was going to transform into a drag queen.

The song he was going to perform was playing on a loop in the background. After the fourth time hearing it, I was ready to launch his computer out the third-story window. Little did I know, I was going to hear it many, many more times before the night was over.

He spent the next few hours getting ready and talking about all the ideas he had for future performances. He told me all the songs he wanted to perform and which ones meant the most to him. He talked about all the outfits he wanted to make once he had the money to afford the material. He talked and talked and talked. Then, he talked some more.

I nodded and tried to follow along as best as I could. He was so excited and passionate talking about drag that I was getting concerned that he wasn't inhaling enough oxygen between words. It made me realize that he probably didn't have anybody else to talk to about his art.

"What does your family think about your drag?" I asked.

"Don't be stupid. They don't even know I'm gay," he replied.

My eyes shot across the mountain of makeup, wigs, and fabric that separated us. I watched him practice lip syncing to

Chaka Khan. The only way to have made that moment gayer was if Lady Gaga came in pissing glitter.

"You're joking," I said.

"No, girl," he said, waving a sassy finger.

"I'm pretty sure they know. They're probably just waiting for you to come out."

"Oh, I could never do that. My parents would kill me."

After a few more hours, Israel was finally finished getting ready. He put on the final touches in his bedroom while I waited with anticipation in the living room. I was ready to see his completed drag queen transformation for the first time. After all the talk (all the talk), after all the hype, I was going to see exactly what Israel was so passionate about.

"You ready?" He shouted from behind the door.

"Ready," I shouted back.

He pressed play on Chaka Khan for at least the ninety-eighth time that night. The door swung open, and he strutted onto the runway that was his living room. I couldn't believe what I was seeing.

Israel shifted his heels across the floor, trying to maintain his balance. His legs quivered like a newborn giraffe falling from the womb. His dress was a beautiful, clumpy black that gave him the sexy shape of a trashcan. It was short enough to give a flirtatious tease of the boxer shorts he wore underneath. He continued strutting toward the overhead light, allowing me to see his completed makeup. His contour was sleek and crisp like skid marks across his cheeks. His foundation, blush, and highlight looked like a talented painter was precise in making sure the colors didn't overlap.

The most important feature of any person was their eyebrows, and Israel really nailed them. From far away, they looked like thick reeds jutting out of a pond of mud. But up close, they looked the same. At the end of the runway, Israel drifted his hand beneath his chin and posed.

"I'm Isadora Devine Manson. What do you think?"

My jaw dropped, staring at the transformation. "You look stunning! You're going to perform like this?"

"Yeah, duh. I didn't spend five hours getting ready to not

perform like this. Why?"

"Oh, just wondering if you were going to have an outfit change or something."

"I almost forgot!" Isadora disappeared into his bedroom, returning with a fabulous tarp that he threw around his arms like a shall. He twirled proudly.

"Now, it's perfect!" I announced.

We could tell we arrived in Downtown L.A. when the stench of urine penetrated the car windows. During the regular nine-to-five day, the city bustled with business people running around to various offices in towering buildings. However, once the sun set, it was an entirely different city.

Isadora swerved around mounds of trash piling throughout the streets. Human feces were scattered along the cracked sidewalks. This was the part of Los Angeles that wasn't shown in the movies. However, we weren't just going to Downtown.

After cruising down a few one-way streets, we found ourselves in Skid Row—the area of Downtown belonging to over two thousand homeless people. Encampments littered the sidewalks, spilling onto the streets. People roamed around like zombies from the Walking Dead with nowhere to go. They had complete disregard for themselves as they strolled in front of oncoming traffic.

We pulled up to the southwest corner of Skid Row.

"This is where we're going?" I asked, warily. I kept my eye on a homeless man violently twitching at the corner.

"Yep. This is Redline," Isadora answered.

We cautiously made our way from the car to an average door that showed no indication of what the venue was. Isadora led me through.

I stepped into the large room that was a stark contrast from Skid Row outside. Redline was a clean, spacious venue that lacked the smell of stale beer and regurgitation that was found in most bars. It was far from being a dive and slightly more classy than a regular bar. It was unlike any bar I had ever been to in either the Inland Empire or WeHo.

The patrons were casual. People wore black and had tattoos and piercings. A lot of the men sported clean beards, and the women wore T-shirts and jeans. There was a subtle vibe to Redline, as if nobody was there trying to impress each other. Instead, people seemed to be genuinely hanging out. The bar was like the cool older cousin of WeHo bars that didn't need to be obnoxiously loud to garner attention.

"You sure this is a gay bar?" I asked Isadora.

Before he could answer, a towering drag queen with a face covered in neon makeup, raced past us toward the bar. He planted his knees on top of a barstool and leaned over toward the bartender. The queen licked his overdrawn lips with what appeared to be an attempt to flirt but just seemed painfully awkward. It was like watching a teenage girl trapped in a man's body.

There were more drag queens on the other side of the venue. Some wore outfits with Spanish flair. Others had a more gothic, alternative appeal. Some queens even had full beards. It was my first time seeing queens in full wardrobe, makeup, and a strong beard protruding from it all. I was accustomed to seeing traditional queens in WeHo and on television—performers with the goal of appearing as feminine as possible. I was surprised to see queens accentuating their masculine features.

"Come here, I want you to meet some people," Isadora said.

"But I hate people," I replied to deaf ears.

He pulled me to a table by the stage to an eclectic group of people, all with impressively manicured eyebrows. I learned that most of them were off-duty drag queens like Luna Lovecock, Scarlett Moon, and Vivian Vicious. Along with them was a female drag queen with bright green hair that introduced herself to me as 'Puzzi Niggr'.

"The show is about to start. I'm going to go backstage," Isadora said.

"Please don't leave me here," I pleaded, not wanting to be left with strangers, but Isadora was already crossing the threshold that divided the performers from people that didn't have their genitals tucked behind them.

"Did you see him on Rupaul's Drag Race? Bitch, even I'm fishier than him," I overheard from a conversation at the table.

"Don't be shady, girl," another voice said.

"I was gagged at his outfit," came from the other side.

I tried to keep up with the multiple conversations bouncing all over the place. I nodded my head, pretending to understand what any of the lingo meant. Everyone was smiling and laughing, but some of the words that came out of their mouths had an edge to them. I couldn't tell if they liked whatever they were talking about or hated it.

As I was getting lost in the labyrinth of conversation, the neon-colored drag queen from the bar hurried over to the table, slamming himself down onto a stool.

"Hi!" He shouted. His face was like a box of Crayola crayons all melted together.

"Hello," I responded.

"I'm Rubella Spreads and you should too!" He shouted, with complete disregard for my personal space. "I know what you're thinking and, yes, I am that pretty."

"Oh, okay," I said.

"Shut up, you big bitch!" A cartoonish voice jabbed at Rubella from across the table. I glanced over to see a pretty, yet handsome, guy with tattoos on his hands. He wore a fang necklace made of stone over his ripped, black shirt. His prominent hairy chest peeked out from beneath the fabric.

"You're just jealous you're not a pretty girl like me," Rubella responded.

"Leave the poor guy alone. You're scaring him."

"A little bit," I admitted.

"Hey," the guy continued, "I don't think we've met yet."

I introduced myself. We were talking a bit when I noticed he didn't speak like the other people at the table. He had a calm demeanor where he didn't shout over people to get his voice heard. He didn't seem in constant need of attention. He was casual, but also had an impressive ability where he could make fun of a person in front of their face without them even knowing it.

"What's your name?" I asked him.

"Pinché Queen," he replied.

"I'm going to assume that's not a birth name."

"It's my drag name."

"You're a drag queen?" I asked, surprised.

"Yes?" He replied, as if it was obvious.

"You just seem so different from everyone else."

He laughed. "Thanks, I think. You should come to one of my shows."

Just as I was about to pull out my phone to get his number, the lights dimmed. A spotlight illuminated the stage. The DJ cut the music as the host commandeered the microphone.

"Ladies and gentlemen, please welcome Imperia!"

A Spanish song rang through the speakers, accompanying a tiny queen onto the stage. His crisp, clean makeup presented him with the fragility of a porcelain doll. The spotlight reflecting off his cheek highlight was blinding. His outfit was like a glamorous 1950s starlet that never had to light their own cigarette.

He lip synced up and down the stage. I had never seen a queen perform a song in Spanish before. In fact, it was the first time I had ever seen a queen perform any song outside of the realm of Beyonce, Britney Spears, or Lady Gaga. The audience was living for it.

As Imperia's performance was concluding, a disheveled boy wearing a bright safety vest wandered into the venue. He carried a large bag, sneaking through the audience to find a seat in front of the stage. Skid Row was an interesting place; I thought it was poetic to see a homeless queer kid attending a drag show.

The kid cheered when the next performer took the stage. Valerie Von Boom made his introduction with high energy. He graced the stage with an erratic fervor. He had a completely different style of drag than his predecessor. Valerie was a black queen with an exquisitely large derriere and toned body that left me wondering if he was biologically male or female.

Valerie pulled out two wands. He struck fire to the ends,

illuminating the entire room. With each twist of his body, the flames kissed his skin. The heat radiated from the wands as he became a whirlwind of danger and beauty, nearly singeing the audience. His body arched and swayed in unison with the flames, proving that drag was so much broader than what I had known.

Throughout the performances, Rubella relentlessly tried to stick his fingers in my ear, grope my leg, and tell me how pretty he was. Normally, I would have gotten annoyed, but it was really inspiring to see a mentally challenged person find an outlet doing drag. I tried my best to remain patient, but the Queen of Crayola was driving me to drink.

"Hey," I called to Pinché. "Want a shot?"

We wandered toward the bar together and ordered shots of tequila.

"What kind of drag do you do? Do you do Spanish songs or do you do the whole fire twirling thing?" I asked.

"My drag is a bit different. I'm more of an unapologetic, in-your-face kind of drag queen."

"Really? You seem like such a calm person."

"That's exactly why my drag character is different. I can show the parts of my personality that aren't always showing."

"Is that why people do drag?" I asked.

"Depends on the person, I guess. Some people enjoy wearing makeup; some people like the attention when doing drag; some just want to express themselves."

I was still unsure why people would want to wear a dress and pretend to sing. I couldn't understand how that was empowering.

"Here, get my number. I'll let you know next time I have a show," Pinché said.

As I pulled out my phone once again, the all too familiar tune of Chaka Khan reverberated through Redline. After listening to it all day, I was conditioned to think of Isadora as soon as it blasted.

"Isadora is performing!"

Pinché and I hurried back to the table before we could exchange numbers.

The ballad played as Isadora sashayed through the threshold of curtains that signified the complete transformation from Israel to Isadora. He strutted across the stage. Israel had never had so many eyes fixated on him, but Isadora seemed to thrive on them.

He glowed beneath the spotlight. Every flaw in his makeup was evident, his outfit was far from polished, and his wig was lackluster, but in that moment none of that mattered. The emotion that exuded from Isadora was enough to captivate everyone. His facial expressions told the story of every word that his lips fluttered to. He graced every inch of the stage as if it had always been his home—as if that was where he belonged. His lips may have been artificial, but the smile was the realest thing I had ever seen.

Isadora drifted down the steps of the stage, into the audience. He engaged with the faces in the crowd, soaking in the adulation. The audience was enchanted as he paraded around. Then, he stopped in front of me.

He turned around, married to the tune of the music, and flashed me a smile I had never seen before. He was showing me a person I had never met—not just the character of Isadora, but the blurred line between fantasy and reality. Isadora emoted a confidence he had never expressed before. He was weightless in a whirl of ecstasy that he created; a world where he could be himself without judgment. He was happy.

He glided back onto the stage, concluding the three minutes. The audience erupted with applause. As was customary at a drag show, people tipped Isadora with dollar bills. While he waved to the crowd, the homeless boy wearing the safety vest handed Isadora a couple of dollars. It was heartwarming to see that even a homeless person appreciated drag enough to contribute.

I waited for Isadora to rejoin us at the table. I was finally warming up to the people around me or, at least, the tequila warmed me up.

Like his name suggested, Rubella would not go away.

"So *pretteh*!" He kept babbling nonsensically.

"Are you trying to say 'pretty'?" I asked.

"So *pretteh*!" He repeated. Rubella and I had apparently developed a bond that I didn't remember agreeing to. He kept trying to get closer and closer. I could feel his breath on my face.

"Damn, Rubella, leave him alone already," Pinché shouted at the neon queen.

"Shut up, Pudgy!" Rubella fired back.

Isadora approached us with his head held high.

"So, what did you think?" He asked, readjusting his falling wig.

"You're not the person I used to know," I admitted.

"I told you," he said.

"And I thought it was amazing that the cute homeless kid tipped you."

"Homeless kid?"

"The boy with the safety vest," I said, pointing.

"Girl!" Isadora laughed. "That's Felony Dodger! He's a drag queen!"

"Oh my god." I shook my head trying to erase the embarrassment from my mind. "Let me buy you a drink so we can forget I said that."

"I wish I could, but I have to go. I have work in a few hours."

"You go to work after you do a show?" I asked.

"Drag is not cheap, girl. I've got to keep working."

We said our goodbyes to everyone. Redline was a fun alternative to the WeHo bars. The LGBT+ community in Downtown seemed welcoming. The diversity was refreshing and everyone seemed more interested in art than the hook-up culture that stereotyped our community. Despite all of that, I doubted that I would ever return to Downtown.

I ran up to Pinché just as my Lyft pulled up.

"I almost forgot to get your number," I told the off-duty queen.

He put it in my phone. I headed outside when I heard the faint, slurred scream of an obnoxious drag queen: "So *pretteh*!"

QUEEN KONG

The sound of the tattoo gun vibrating against my skin filled the tiny parlor. The pain was rapid. The pain was sharp. The pain was consistent. But the pain of physical scarification was nothing compared to emotional wounds. Endorphins soothed my mind.

Getting ink etched into my body was becoming my newest addiction. The intense euphoria of pain caused by something so deeply personal was validating. It was like reflecting on a tribulation in life and accepting the change forever. The ink would remind me of the trials I went through —whether they were good or bad didn't matter. What mattered was that I came out of them a different person.

The tattoo artist wreaked of weed. She was a hippy with unwashed hair but radiated positive vibes. She dipped the cluster of needles into red ink.

I never believed I would get a color tattoo. All my previous ones were strictly black. But, like my other tattoos, this one had a powerful meaning.

I was eighteen years old when Proposition 8—the ban of

same-sex marriage—had passed in California. It was the first election I had ever voted in. I truly believed that there was no way Prop. 8 would pass. But, alas, I was introduced to my first taste of the harsh reality of politics.

After the results were announced, a dejected LGBT+ community congregated at the West Hollywood Park, along with lawyers in the case, politicians, and celebrity allies. I was there on that somber day. I stood with my queer brothers and sisters with tears openly streaming our faces. What was usually a park full of queer families during the day and people galavanting at night, was filled with the overwhelming sadness of hundreds of community members.

Speakers tried to raise our spirits by saying we would continue to fight for our rights. They declared we would regroup and fight back even harder. However, it was impossible not to feel the disappointment of not being recognized as an equal in the eyes of society. It was a devastating day for all of us.

Around the same time, I sported the red shirt and khaki pants that signified working as a Target employee. One day, I was hiding in a private corner of the building, consuming a bag of Hot Cheetos that I definitely didn't pay for. As I was enjoying the spicy delectable, two of my coworkers found me.

"What are you doing back here?" Alfonso asked with an adorably gay lisp.

"Nothing," I replied, licking the red chip dust from my fingers.

"Got anymore?" José asked.

I handed them each their own bag since there was no point in sharing when the supply was unlimited. As we were getting paid to hang out, Alfonso's phone went off with a Lady Gaga song.

"Really?" José asked him.

"Oh my god, have you listened to her new album? It's, like, so amazing," Alfonso said.

"Do you have to be so gay?" José asked.

"Why do you always make fun of me for being gay?" Alfonso returned. "Why don't you ever talk about him being gay?"

He pointed at me. My red-stained fingers froze after stuffing a Cheeto into my mouth. The slow crunch of the chip filled the silence with a deafening sound. I had never been outed before. My heart fell into my stomach with the spicy snack.

"Because he doesn't act gay," José answered.

I was partially relieved that I wasn't outed, considering he apparently already knew.

"But you," José continued. "You act so gay. You prance around everywhere and listen to Lady Gaga. I don't care if you're gay, but don't do that shit in front of me."

The disappointment on Alfonso's face was crushing. His usually bubbly personality burst. It was despairing to witness the rejection. However, it was an opportunity for me to stand up for someone that was not only a brother to me in the LGBT+ community but also a friend. It was a chance to stand together and not let society divide us.

Instead, I turned around finally deciding to work. I didn't say anything. I didn't turn back toward them. I could feel Alfonso's disappointment behind me, but that paled in comparison to the disappointment I had in myself. I was so terrified of compromising being accepted that I let someone else feel isolated.

A few days after, I sat in the chair at the tattoo parlor. After the artist finished with the red, she dipped the gang of needles into the orange ink. Then the yellow. My blood trickled down the side of my arm. She wiped it then went back to etching in green followed by blue. Finally she added purple.

My raw skin was burning with thousands of little holes, but a satisfied smile crossed my face looking at the completed piece. The colors of the rainbow lined up within the outline of a triangle on the top of my wrist. The rainbow represented the colors of the LGBT+ flag. The triangle was my connection to the lives that were sacrificed before me. It was a symbol used by the Nazis for queers in concentration camps. Eventually, the triangle symbol was taken back by the LGBT+ community and used to represent a "safe zone"—a place where queer people were welcomed.

I decided on those symbols to mark myself as queer. I chose to scar my body so I would never be able to hide my identity, no matter how dire a situation may have become. It was my homage to my community but, more personally, it was to remind myself to never hide who I was.

Like my gay brothers that succumbed to the Nazis, I was marked. However, instead of it being a symbol of shame, I was proud to wear a mark that the LGBT+ community had reclaimed as a symbol of safety.

*　　　*　　　*

"My dick is stuck!" I screamed, zipping up my pants eerily close to my flesh.

"I don't care; let's go!" Pinché pulled my arm, dashing across 6th street. We rounded the corner, running into a line that wrapped around the block.

"Holy balls." My eyes widened. "We're never getting in."

Pinché's tattooed hand continued pulling me. We skated all the way to the front, bypassing the resentful faces waiting in line, where Pinché shared some words with the door person. I tried to not look back at everyone glaring at us.

"Are you coming in or what?" Pinché asked, disappearing into a hallway.

"Are we really going to be those people?" I asked.

"You want to wait in line?"

I shook my head.

"Bitch, I'm a celebrity; let's go!" Pinché responded with possible sarcasm.

We made our way through a cold, empty corridor that looked like a secret passageway rather than an entrance to a club. We ascended a flight of stairs. Looming at the top was a colossal poster of a gorilla shoving a bottle of poppers into her nose. Above the beast, in bright pink letters, read the words "Queen Kong". We breezed by admissions, finally entering the venue.

A gust of human humidity smashed into me. Queen Kong was packed. Everyone was shoulder-to-shoulder or bulge-to-bulge. There were big, burly men with impressive beards. There were short guys with hulking muscles. Old guys wore leather. Young women wore Bauhaus shirts. Others wore nothing more than straps and chains. Bearded drag queens and packing drag kings were scattered throughout.

The people were unlike any I had seen at a single club before. Everyone had such a different style and body type that I wasn't quite sure how they were meshing so well together. It was the exact opposite of WeHo, where people prided themselves on fitting into a mold. Queen Kong was like a land of proud misfits. Instead of being cast out of the mainstream, the Kong crowd chose to avoid it.

She Wants Revenge pounded out of the speakers when a tall drag queen marched by me. He was covered in nothing but tribal makeup and a tight, black thong that left no excess room for his junk. His body was covered with tattoos and piercings. The word "FAGGOT" was inked across his stomach in bold letters.

Then, another even taller queen passed with monstrous, disheveled blue hair. His boots were reminiscent of an exotic dancer, but he had the makeup of a creature rising from the depths of hell. I learned that Frankie Doom was appreciative of being compared to a demonic stripper. His breastplate bounced as he clomped away.

Sweat rolled down my neck from the overheated bodies around me.

"I need a drink, bad," I told Pinché.

We zigzagged through the eclectic crowd, finally reaching a side of the bar we could squeeze into. As we waited for the sweet nectar of Jack Daniels, a boisterous, terrorizing voice next to us shouted at the bartender. I gazed over to see a drag queen that looked like the star of a new Tyler Perry movie, Madea Gets Gang-Banged.

"Hey, henny!" The character screeched at Pinché.

"Hey, bitch!" He hugged the queen then turned to me. "This is Meatball."

"Hello," I choked out, unimpressively. I extended my hand as a gesture, but Meatball reached around and palmed my entire ass with one hand.

"Oh," I stammered at the flattering harassment.

Before Meatball released my buttocks, he discharged an uncivilized noise I could only imagine an animal would make in a dying orgasm. "Hhhhm… Que, que, que, que, yes, yes!"

Not a moment too soon, the bartender returned with our drinks. Pinché and I departed from the ever-charming Meatball, proceeding on our journey. We pushed our way to an adjacent room where a stage loomed beneath the shadows of sparkling red curtains. As we squeezed through people, I could feel strangers' sweat drip onto me and into my drink. For each person I contorted myself past, my drink spilled over. When we finally reached the front of the stage, my entire drink was empty before I could even take a sip.

"Goddamn it, I have to get another one," I told Pinché.

"The show is about to start," he warned.

A drum roll rattled the venue followed by an introduction of trumpets. The stage curtains shook then shot open, revealing two queens dressed in identical makeup and outfits.

"Welcome everybody to Queen Kong!" The shorter of the two said.

"We are the Boulet Brothers!"

The crowd roared as the monstrous, but polished, characters spoke. The queens carried a celebrity air with them. Their energy was grander than the stage they stood on. Their charisma and ethereal appearance radiated an aura like leaders of a cult. Whatever blood-infused Kool-Aid they were spewing to us, we were eagerly drinking.

"Do you know them?" I asked Pinché.

"Everyone knows them. I've never performed Queen Kong, but everyone knows the Boulet Brothers," he answered.

The Brothers introduced the first act. An adult-sized chicken puppet with vehemently red feathers bobbed onto the stage. I almost couldn't believe what I was witnessing. The puppet—Miss Fuego—"lip synced" to a song in Spanish and… danced?

"I'm way too sober for this," I lamented. "I'll be right back."

I pulled away from Pinché, moving through the sweaty crowd. I was finally able to squeeze into an empty pocket next to a hidden bar.

"Hey, I like your tattoos," a feminine voice danced over the music toward me.

I turned to see a short guy with perfectly coiffed hair. His angelic smile produced a single dimple on the left side of his face. Below his right eye was a tiny tattoo of a crescent moon. He leaned against the bar with a commanding femininity.

"Thanks," I replied, awkwardly.

"Not a lot of people would get a rainbow tattooed on their arm," he continued.

"That was kind of my reasoning."

"I'm Gabriel."

The innocent gleam in Gabriel's eyes felt like a mesmerizing trap. Like the song of a siren, except he didn't need to make a single sound. I had to end the conversation, however. Not only because I didn't know how to react to someone as intriguing as him, but also because I still hadn't received my results from the clinic yet. I wasn't sure about my status and I didn't want to tease myself by talking to Gabriel. Sure we could have been extra careful if the night even led to sex but, let's face it, who knew how much we were going to drink or how many bad decisions we would make.

"I have to find my friends now," I told him.

"Oh," he replied.

"Well, let me get your number," I said, feeling bad for leaving so abruptly.

After getting his number, I wandered around realizing my mission was unintentionally aborted. Gabriel's gaze made my brain weak; I had completely forgotten to grab a drink. I made a detour for the other bar when I stumbled upon a wrap-around balcony full of tables, vendors, and people gasping for air.

Sitting at one of the tables was a compact-sized human with a curly, purple mane of hair. I had met Jessica before, but all I could remember was that she was the unofficial promoter of drag queens. She attended most shows and kept social media buzzing with videos of performances she captured. She also talked a mile a minute, and I was far too sober to pretend to care about the words she would say. I avoided eye contact as best as I could until she noticed me.

"Hey! Hey, come over here!" She hissed at me. "You look stressed."

"The amount of people here is a bit overwhelming," I admitted. "I hate people and there's a lot of them."

"Same. You can sit here and talk shit about them with me."

That was a mighty proposition, but I was on a quest. I turned around to face the crowd engulfing the bar. People continued filing into Queen Kong. The effort to push my way anywhere required determination beyond my energy level. I admitted defeat and reluctantly joined Jessica.

"See that queen over there?" She pointed. "One of his ass pads is practically touching his breastplate. He's like a bucket of chicken with pieces in every direction."

I laughed at the casual insult.

"It's okay," she assured me. "Most of the queens here are my friends."

Jessica shouted at the queen to come over.

"Fix your damn pad. Your ass is looking like a titty," she demanded, like a mom straightening out her child before a performance. She helped the queen maneuver their padding and sent him on his way again. This happened a couple more times with various queens. Jessica fixed hairlines, tightened corsets, and gave offensive pep talks. She was like the Michelle Visage of L.A.'s underground drag scene.

"Damn, I knew I could feel a rumbling in the building," Jessica said between sips of her drink.

I glanced over to see Pinché marching up to us.

"Oh my god, you're awful," I told Jessica.

"Hey, you Grimace-looking bitch," Pinché fired back, flicking Jessica's purple hair. Then he turned to me, "C'mon, the second part of the show is starting."

"I still need a damn drink," I said, having withdrawals.

"You can have some of mine," Jessica offered.

She was like an angel from God. I was finally going to put my liver to work and give my insides the warm, fuzzy feeling they deserved. I put my hand around her condensation-soaked cup and moved the straw toward my lips.

"They make them strong here," Jessica mentioned. "It's almost pure vodka."

I stopped the straw centimeters from my lips. My face dropped with disappointment. There was a specific alcohol taste that brought back terrifying memories of drinking out of mason jars all night then passing out naked behind a stranger's toilet. Vodka was that alcohol. I wasn't going to make the same mistake three times, despite how desperate I was. I handed Jessica back her drink.

"Let's go, Tito is about to perform!" Pinché pulled me from the balcony back into the main room. He shoved his way through people, managing to stop by the bar like a drive-through. He shouted at the bartender and, within seconds, a Jack and Coke was in my hand.

"Here!" Pinché yelled. "Now stop being a whiney bitch."

In that moment, he could have called me anything he wanted; it wouldn't have fazed me. All that mattered, was that I had a drink better than the blood of Christ in my hand. I could finally proceed with permanently damaging my liver, nervous system, and life. I took a sip and floated into the sanctuary of intoxication.

We made our way to the stage just in time for the act. The spotlight lingered as the red curtains ruffled. Music crescendoed throughout the venue. All conversations in the building ceased as everyone turned their attention toward the stage.

A mythical being emerged from the curtains. Tito wasn't a drag queen, but he was definitely a performer. A muscular, hairy man with a full beard, Tito shook and shimmied across the stage with the flexibility of a ballerina and the strength of a professional wrestler. He projected an unreal mixture of femininity and masculinity that captured the essence of not only what it meant to be a performer but of what it meant to be human.

His charisma was like Freddie Mercury, intensified by the sleek, black leather straps that wrapped his arms, shoulders, and pelvis. Across his eyes was a thin, black mask that added a sexy mystique. His height was shorter than mine, but his presence was larger than life. I was paralyzed by the performance. I stared in awe as the mystical creature embodied divinity. I was convinced that I was staring at God.

The music kept building. Tito moved faster and faster, dancing across the stage. His momentum escalated. His movements snapped. I clutched my drink. There was barely room for us to stand. Every misfit in the audience was pressed together sharing the same moment. Pinché and I were side-by-side. I glanced at him with an undying appreciation, love, and gratitude for introducing me to an underground world of queer art that I only dreamed existed.

The godly being continued onstage. Tito's powerful chest heaved for air. As the music came crashing, he leaped into the air, landing in a climactic pose beneath the spotlight. Cannons of confetti and glitter launched overhead, raining down on all the queers packing Queen Kong. The roar of the crowd was deafening. Everyone and everything was covered with confetti.

I looked down to see glitter coating my entire body. I stared at my rainbow tattoo shimmering beneath the lights. A raw, messy feeling of comfort engulfed me. This was where I belonged. I looked over again at Pinché.

"Thank you," I whispered. "You've changed my life."

The glitter in my drink heavily outweighed the whiskey, but that didn't matter. I brought the cup to my mouth and proudly drank the Jack, Coke, and glitter.

WEPA! WEPA! WEPA!

"**G**irl, grab the nails!" Isadora shouted.

"I'm trying!" I shouted back, fumbling with an assortment of bags.

He ran across the street, lifting his dress to avoid tripping. He yanked a suitcase full of makeup, energy drinks, and other drag queen essentials. He had already taped his chest, creating the illusion of voluptuous breasts. His face was already painted and his outfit was intact. But there was no time for him to put on heels. His chanclas slapped the pavement.

"We're going to be late!"

"I'm coming! I'm coming!" I yelled.

It was the first night of the Wepa competition at Faultline but, more importantly, it was the first time Isadora was part of a competition.

He had been building his name in Los Angeles for the better part of a year and was garnering the attention of enough drag queens to get booked for shows. However, this show was different. It was a weekly competition that would span the entire summer with the winner earning paid bookings and a substantial cash prize.

"Girl, if you make me late to the first show and I get disqualified—"

"Me?! You've been at my apartment for six hours getting ready. Half of those you spent babbling about the convict you blew the other night."

After Isadora helped me back on my feet, I was able to secure a job that paid well enough for me to move into my own apartment. I started paying off my credit card debt and vowed to never eat another Subway sandwich again. I was truly living the life of the rich and famous—even paying for my own Wi-Fi.

Isadora had since moved back in with his family. His parents still didn't know about him moonlighting as a drag queen. Instead of getting ready at his house, Isadora would drive his beat-up car to the closest park, click on the weak overhead lights, and put on his makeup using the rearview mirror before every gig.

When I found that out, I offered him my apartment to use as a giant walk-in closet anytime he needed to get into drag. It was the least I could do after all that he had helped me with. Without hesitation, he took full advantage.

"Tristan hit me up," Isadora said, as he drove us across Melrose.

"Did you respond?" I asked.

"Of course. He was my best friend."

"You've been doing amazing with your drag. You sure you want to invite that chaos back into your life?"

He took a long drag of his cigarette before making a sharp right turn. He pulled up to the corner of Melrose and Vermont, skidding into a tiny parking lot.

"We're on time!" Isadora praised himself.

"Your wig isn't even on, you don't have nails, and you're wearing chanclas!" I reminded him.

"Well, maybe if you stopped talking and helped me!"

"Don't blame this on me."

"Oh my god, did you bring the nails?"

"Yes?"

I had never offered to be any kind of assistant. All I

wanted to do was collect drink tickets and blackout during the performances so I could look back and assume the queens were really good. Yet, there I was, rummaging around the floor of the car, sifting through empty hairspray cans and fast-food wrappers, searching for plastic nails I could have sworn I remembered to bring.

"Don't you have gloves to wear?" I asked.

"You forgot the nails?! How could you—"

"Got 'em!" I triumphantly raised the tiny pieces of plastic.

I rushed to help glue the nails onto Isadora's trembling hands. His voice shook when he spoke. I had never seen him nervous before. I felt like a mom dropping off their kid on the first day of school. Except my kid was a man in a dress, and I was a mom that wrecked lines of Adderall for breakfast.

"You're going to do great," I said.

Isadora smiled. "Thank you. Next time, we'll be early."

I hoped there would be a next time. Isadora's drag was improving, but he was still far from the same caliber as other local queens. All I could hope was for him to not be eliminated first in the competition. As long as he made it passed the first round, the experience would be worth having.

The competition began, and the queens were introduced one-by-one, performing a song of their choice. Among them was seasoned queen Britney Shears and an up-and-coming Anya Body. The talent pool was impressive. The girls brought their A-game, but none could be compared to Dayshawna Rose.

Dayshawna was a humble, black queen that proved his worth onstage. As soon as his Beyoncé song hit, Dayshawna burst with high energy. The crowd erupted in response. The High-Desert Queen leaped off the stage, jumped on tables, and death-dropped. It was impossible not to be captivated.

The competition was already going to be fierce, but Dayshawna was on the next level. Any small chance of Isadora advancing to the later stages of the competition disappeared as the Beyoncé song came to a close. Isadora wasn't capable of death-drops or jumping on tables. He was a proud big girl and performed like one.

Isadora emerged from backstage when his music hit. Small pockets of the crowd lit up with cheers. Some of his friends and drag sisters were in attendance. If nothing else, he had an impressive support system compared to any other competitor.

I was enamored by Isadora gliding across the stage. He emoted the song with pure allure. All his anxiety completely disappeared. It was difficult to believe that, only ten minutes prior, he was shaking in the parking lot. As soon as the spotlight was on him, he was able to shut out any kind of doubt. Isadora got lost in his art. Most importantly, he was enjoying the moment.

He pulled fans out of his impressive cleavage. With every crack of a fan, he dramatized a sass that the crowd ate up. CRACK. He tossed the fan then pulled out another one. CRACK. He tossed it again and pulled out more. His G-sized faux-breasts were like a black hole of accessories. It was a completely different type of performance than the rest of the competitors. Isadora didn't do handstands or cartwheels, but he entertained the audience with outrageousness, attitude, and ridiculous humor. At the end of his performance, I let out a sigh of relief realizing that I was holding my breath the entire time.

Robbie Osa, the host of the competition, called all the queens back to the stage so the judges could deliver their critiques. The queens each received a few points of praise as well as criticism. Then it came to Dayshawna Rose.

"Dayshawna," Robbie began, "girl, you killed it. You brought the high energy and owned it. You are the winner of the first round!"

The crowd cheered. I reluctantly joined them. I couldn't deny that Dayshawna deserved the victory. No matter how much we needed him to be eliminated, it was clear that he was there to stay.

Finally, it was time for the judges to give their feedback to Isadora. He humbly stepped forward. I inched my way toward the bar getting ready to either buy him a consolation drink or a victory drink. I held my breath again.

"Isadora," Robbie began, "you missed out on a critical point of your outfit. You have a bracelet on, but that's the only piece of jewelry. You're a drag queen. You need to dress like one."

I bought a Vodka and Red Bull for Isadora. It was time for a consolation drink until Robbie continued speaking.

"However, usually when a queen picks an emotional song —like the one you chose tonight—they don't know how to convey the emotion with their face. But you were giving us all the emotion, honey. You made us feel the song and your passion. You are safe from elimination."

Isadora's friends, drag sisters, and new fans cheered in agreement. His focused expression transformed into an ear-to-ear grin. The consolation drink in my hand instantly turned into a celebration drink. He didn't get eliminated first, and that's all I could have hoped for.

A few people stopped Isadora to take pictures before he made his way toward me.

"Congratulations," I said to him.

"I didn't win," Isadora replied.

"You didn't lose."

Dayshawna descended the stage. He strode up to Isadora with an elegant demeanor.

"You did great, girl," Dayshawna said.

"Of course he did," I interrupted. "And you really nailed that Beyoncé. And the death-drop. And the voguing. I've never seen that done before. Ever. At any drag show."

Dayshawna flashed me a smile. I was unsure if it was genuine, or if he was confident enough to take the high road and not engage with my shady sarcasm.

"Thank you," Isadora said to the High-Desert Queen before I could open my mouth again.

It was going to be a competitive summer, but Isadora and I were looking forward to it. We would see Dayshawna in the next round.

✳   ✳   ✳

I shoved a straw in my nose, inhaling a thick line of powder off my living room table. The particles entered my body with a sharpness I had never felt before and never wanted to feel again. It felt like I snorted a line of glass and every shard was shredding my insides, all the way to my brain. I released a guttural growl of pain.

"Holy balls, why does Molly hurt so much?!" I yelled, as I did another line.

"Maybe you shouldn't snort it," Rubella answered, tossing a pill into his mouth and washing it down with a Screwdriver.

"I don't trust swallowing pills. You don't know when it's going to hit. At least when you snort something, you know exactly when it's going to kick in."

"And when is that?"

"Ah, Christ!" I bellowed, taking another line. "Is it supposed to hurt this much?"

"Probably not."

We finished the drugs and the drinks before calling a Lyft. We were on our way to Club Ripples in Long Beach. It probably wasn't the wisest decision to get that intoxicated before getting into a car for an hour-long drive, but we weren't the poster boys for good decisions.

We were sitting in the car for what already felt like forever but was probably only ten minutes, when I got a text message from Gabriel—the guy with the crescent moon tattoo I had met at Queen Kong.

"Have you ever messed around with someone HIV positive?" I asked Rubella.

"Where did that come from?"

I was reluctant to talk about anything as personal as the possibility of contracting a disease, but the anticipation of not knowing my status continued creating an unparalleled anxiety in my mind. I needed to talk to someone.

"This guy I want to like keeps texting me. He wants to hang out, but I've been putting it off because I don't know my status. I don't know what to do."

"You could hang out with him and not have sex," Rubella suggested.

"People do that?" I said somewhat jokingly. I showed him a picture of Gabriel to prove just how difficult it would be to not have sex with him.

"So *pretteh*!"

"What? What is that?" I asked.

"'So *pretteh*?' I never told you that story?" He asked, not waiting for a response. "One time, I was having sex with this guy from behind—I think he was mentally challenged—and as I was thrusting, he looked over his shoulder, straight into my eyes and yelled 'so *pretteh*'!"

The Lyft driver abruptly pulled the car over on a dark street in an unfamiliar city.

"I have to drop you guys off here," the driver said.

"I don't think we're anywhere near Long Beach," I replied.

"Something came up and I can't take you down there."

"Oh. Okay…"

The Queen of Crayola and I got out of the car. We watched the Lyft driver speed away as we surveyed the street in the middle of nowhere. It was empty both ways. Only a handful of street lights kept us company. I wasn't sure if the driver didn't want to drive the distance to Long Beach, or if he was annoyed by our conversation. Maybe he was uncomfortable with Rubella breathing down his neck in an attempt to flirt. Regardless, we stood in the middle of the street hoping the next Lyft we called would find us.

"I think the Molly is kicking in," Rubella announced.

We shivered waiting in the cold for another ten minutes. The Molly had an incredible effect on Rubella. He couldn't (or wouldn't) stop talking no matter how much I pleaded. He babbled about his childhood traumas or what he ate for lunch or something equally pointless. Mercifully, another driver picked us up.

Not learning his lesson from the previous ride, Rubella kept spitting words out of his mouth. Some of them were questions, some were attempts to seduce the driver whose face we couldn't even see, others were partial sentences that never completed a coherent thought. All I wanted was to make it to

Club Ripples, but the obnoxious queen was ruining our chances and my life.

"Where are we?" I asked, staring out the window.

We somehow ended up next to the Queen Mary in the Long Beach Harbor. We were definitely in the right city but not in the right direction of the club. After a few U-turns, dead ends, and more unsolicited Rubella sex stories, we made it to the club.

Rubella leaped out of the car, running into the venue with inhuman energy. I followed at mortal speed. As soon as I entered, I ran into Piper.

"You made it!" She shouted.

"You're here early," I replied.

"I didn't want to be late to my first drag show. The flier said nine, but it hasn't started yet."

"Drag queen time," I informed her.

"What's that?" She asked.

"It's like Pacific or Eastern time, except four hours behind."

Piper was incredibly heterosexual. It wasn't her fault, though. She was not blessed with the amazing genes the majority of us at Club Ripples were blessed with. Regardless, everyone welcomed her. I paraded the breeder around, introducing her to Luna Lovecock, Valerie Von Boom, and other drag queens.

"Hey, you filthy whore!" A voice shouted from across the room.

We turned to see the purple-haired gremlin.

"This is Jessica," I told Piper. "She's awful and judgmental on the outside, but deep, deep down inside she's also trash."

"Do you see that lady's jeans over there?" Jessica said, proving my point.

A middle-aged woman with a bedazzled T-shirt that read "Hot" danced in the middle of the room. The very bottom of her mom jeans were cut into strings so that, when she twirled, the fabric would rise like the swings at a carnival.

"I bet she was really excited to wear those tonight," Jessica continued. "She was probably like 'I'm going to wear my going-out jeans tonight'."

"I don't get it," Piper replied. "Those jeans are pretty cool."

Jessica and I engaged in a synchronized eye roll at Piper's uncontrollable hetero-ness. I didn't mind that she was straight; I just wished she didn't do it in front of me. Before we could be disappointed in anymore of Piper's life choices, Robbie Osa wandered up to us.

"Hey!" Robbie hugged me.

"What are you doing here?" I asked. "Especially out of drag."

"Girl, tonight is my night off from hosting the Wepa competition. I need this."

"Same. That competition is stressing me out and I'm not even in it." We laughed in agreement before Robbie continued toward the bar.

"So," Piper began, "do they call each other 'girl' even when they're not in drag?"

I laughed. I had never thought about how strange that word might sound to people outside of the LGBT+ community.

"Gender is pretty open in our community. 'Girl' is like saying 'dude' or 'bro'."

"Oh… Okay, girl."

I cringed at the sound of her using the word. I knew she was trying to be funny or understanding, but it sounded like nails on a chalkboard. I was happy she was trying to educate herself, but straight people should have stuck to their own cultural norms like gender roles and missionary position.

After dancing for a few hours, watching a drag show, and wandering around the massive venue, we all congregated once more just as last call was approaching. We stood around Jessica's table, swaying in our drunkenness.

"Has anyone seen Rubella?" I asked.

The Queen of Crayola stumbled up to us double-fisting Screwdrivers.

"You're a mess," I told him.

"Does anyone want this?" Jessica asked, holding up a

free-drink ticket. "It's the last one."

"Why don't you use it?" Luna asked.

"I can't," Jessica burped. She tried to hand the ticket off.

"I can't either," Luna passed the ticket.

"I'm already wasted," Valerie replied, trying to give it to Rubella.

Rubella couldn't articulate words, but he shook his head, returning to the two drinks already in his hands.

I grabbed the drink ticket. I stared at its magnificent beauty like the precious ring to Gollum or the golden ticket to Willy Wonka's factory. I tried to focus my vision. I steadily placed it back onto the table.

"Are we so messed up, that all of us said 'no' to a free drink?"

It was a shameful moment in our drinking careers, but it was probably the best decision any of us had ever made.

The lights came on in the venue signifying closing time. Piper thanked me for introducing her to my world before she left. The rest of us were set to call Lyfts when I gazed across the street. Beyond the road and a field of sand, rested a calm bay.

"The ocean is across the street," I pointed out. "There's no way we're not going over there."

None of us were ready for the night to end. So Rubella, Valerie, Luna, Robbie, Jessica, and I made our way toward the West Coast water. Valerie and I sprinted in a race, trying to expel the energy we had left. He had completely removed his drag and proved that he was just as athletic without a dress. We struggled to catch our breaths while the rest of the group strolled over.

"Where's Rubella?" I asked, as it was becoming the theme of the night.

We looked back to find the off-duty drag queen passed out on a slab of concrete in the parking lot.

"We may have pre-gamed a bit too hard." I answered everyone's question before they even asked. However, I was surprised that Rubella crashed so soon after taking all the Molly earlier in the night.

"I want a rematch," I told Valerie.

"You're trippin' if you think I'm running again."

I jumped on his back. "Either race me or carry me!"

"Get your scrawny—"

Before he could finish his sentence, Luna came barreling toward us with his hands outstretched. My legs were locked in Valerie's arms, leaving no way for me to protect myself. Luna shoved us with full force. Valerie and I toppled over, bringing chaos to the calm waters of Long Beach. The icy bay chilled my skin and soaked my already too-tight jeans. My penis ran inside me and would not soon return.

Robbie was smart enough to strip off his pants for fear of getting pushed into the ocean with his clothes. Luna, Valerie, and I followed suit, although my clothes were already a lost cause. Jessica howled from the shore.

I wondered how my life led me to that moment standing in my underwear in the ocean with a group of drag queens. For the first time since moving to Los Angeles, I felt like I found a group of LGBT+ people that I could connect with. I gazed around appreciating the moment when I couldn't help feeling that something was missing.

I turned toward the parking lot, but I couldn't see Rubella. Through the haze of the morning fog, the six-foot-tall queen sprinted toward us, tossing his pants into the sand.

"So *pretteh*!" He cried, crashing into the ocean with us.

We scrambled around the bay water as a completed group. We talked shit to each other, took pictures, and tried to drown Valerie—typical things friends did.

After realizing the water was full of industrial machine runoff, we trekked across the sandy terrain, carrying our drenched clothes. Once we got to the parking lot, everyone jumped into their respective cars and headed home, leaving Rubella and me stuck in Long Beach waiting for a Lyft.

I spent the next fifteen minutes struggling to get my pants back on. They were covered in sand and soaking wet. The smell of polluted West Coast ocean runoff saturated them. They refused to cooperate. It was going to take a small miracle to get them back on.

When the Lyft finally arrived, Rubella fell into the backseat passing out immediately. I threw my pants next to him along with my shoes. I hopped in wearing only briefs to cover my shriveled genitalia.

"Please don't leave us on the side of the road," I begged the driver.

*   *   *

"My sister found out I do drag," Isadora told me, while he put on the finishing touches of his makeup before we had to head to Faultline for the competition.

"What?! How? What did she say? Are you okay?" I demanded.

"Relax," he laughed. "She thinks it's cool."

"How are you so calm about it?! Just last year, your family didn't even know you were gay."

"C'mon, girl. I'm pretty sure my family knows. Listen to my voice."

"You think your parents know you do drag?"

"I'm not sure. I mean, I leave the house with suitcases a couple nights a week and come back late in the morning. Even if they did know, they wouldn't say anything. Like, they would probably ignore it rather than openly hate it."

"The people that love you shouldn't have to ignore parts of you," I told him.

"It is what it is," he said, avoiding the conversation.

"But your sister is okay with it?"

"Hell yeah. She helps me with my makeup. She even wants to come to one of my shows."

"That's awesome!"

"Oh my god, we're late!" Isadora shouted.

It was the second round of the Wepa competition, but it was feeling identical to the first. Isadora sped his way toward the venue while I hung on to the car door for my life. He smoked his routine cigarette; the flame coming dangerously close to his synthetic wig.

"You know, this would be a terrible time to get pulled

over," I said, staring at his gown and boldly painted face. "Imagine having a mugshot like this or being in a holding cell."

Isadora shot me a look.

He skidded into the parking lot with only minutes to spare.

"You got the nails?" He asked, putting on his eyelashes.

"Of course," I answered, searching for the damn nails.

"Glue them on right this time. I need to look perfect. I'm having a special guest here tonight."

"Is your sister coming?" I asked, hopeful.

"Hurry up, it's about to start." He shifted his high heels out of the car. "Next time we'll be early."

I wandered around Faultline, waiting for the Wepa competition to begin. I tried to enjoy the night as much as possible, since I didn't feel like we would be back for the next round.

I was ecstatic Isadora didn't get eliminated first, and there would be no shame in going home second, especially with the caliber of the other competitors. Isadora was still a newer queen that had a lot to learn before he had a chance at winning a competition. Also, there was Dayshawna Rose.

That week's performance was a team challenge, where each competitor paired up to do a duet. Dayshawna and his partner unsurprisingly wowed the audience with their high-energy style. Without a doubt, the High-Desert Queen outshined his partner, stealing the show.

Next was Isadora and his partner, Britney Shears. It was an uncharacteristic performance for the Queen of Emotion. Isadora wore an elegant beauty pageant gown with a towering up-do to match. Glamorous jewelry shimmered from all over his body. He and Britney danced and swayed in sync like two princesses on parade. It was a stark contrast from seeing Isadora devour an entire pizza only an hour earlier. He was living the fantasy of class and luxury onstage. I was thankful he chose Britney Shears as a partner. The two worked well together, and it could only benefit Isadora to work with such an experienced queen.

I scanned the venue hoping to spot Isadora's sister, but

she was nowhere to be seen. Then, I heard a familiar shrill voice calling me from across the room.

"Hey, puta! Give me a hug," Tristan rasped at me. "I haven't seen you in years and you're not even going to say 'hi'?"

"What are you doing here?" I asked, shocked.

"I came to see my girl, Isadora, duh!"

"You know he's been doing really well by himself?" I tried to politely point out that Isadora didn't need him around.

"Of course he's doing well. Even though I could do better. But I don't want to do drag," he snapped.

I returned to watching the performance when Tristan leaned on my arm.

"So, did you miss me? You missed me didn't you? Want to fuck?"

"What the hell, Tristan!?"

"I'm sober now, you know?"

"There's a beer in your hand."

He laughed. "Not beer sober. But like liquor. No more liquor. Or Meth."

A photographer was weaving around the audience, taking pictures of the competition when Tristan pulled him over.

"Hey, take my picture." He posed. "Do you do private pics? How much do you charge? Can I suck your dick for pictures?"

The photographer awkwardly turned away, returning his focus on the competition.

The competitors were brought back onto the stage. I was glad Isadora stepped out of his comfort zone for the elegant performance. Regardless of the results, I was proud of him.

"Ladies and gentlemen," Robbie Osa began, "tonight's winning team is Britney Shears and Isadora Manson!"

The crowd cheered and applauded.

"However," Robbie continued, "there can only be one winner each night. So tonight's individual winner is… Isadora!"

The applause were deafening. I was stunned. Isadora graciously accepted the victory and soaked in the adulation of the crowd.

"Maybe he does have a chance," I whispered to myself.

Isadora stepped off the stage. People in the audience raced up to congratulate him. I watched as Tristan shoved the people away to get to Isadora.

"Look, bitch—I'm here!" Tristan shouted.

I marched up to pull him away.

"Sorry, I didn't know he was coming," I said.

"It's okay," Isadora responded. "I invited him."

T-PARTY

I stood in a bedroom of a house somewhere in the Inland Empire. In the center of the room was a neatly made bed with an almost impossible amount of methamphetamine piled on it. Across from me was a lesbian with her hand gripped around a gun. I was staring into the barrel. It was a fun night.

*   *   *

"Why don't we ever party east of here?" I asked Spoons, as I got into the passenger seat of his car.

"I don't know," Spoons replied. "L.A. is always fun, but I've heard of some decent house parties in the Inland Empire. Plus, Stephanie lives around there, and I know she has a gay brother for you. We can meet up with them after."

"First of all, this is boys' night out. We're going out to drink and hang. No hooking up tonight. Second, just because someone is gay doesn't mean I'm automatically going to be attracted to them."

My eighteen-year-old self hated how ignorant everyone

was about LGBT+ people. I was still learning about myself, but I already knew that there were some painfully ugly queers in the world, and that I should never commit to meeting someone based solely on the fact that they were gay.

I cracked open a fresh bottle of Jack Daniels.

"Don't drink too much—you're driving us back," Spoons warned.

I paused before breaking into laughter. Spoons joined knowing full well that we were going to play the "you're slightly less drunk than me" game later to decide who would drive. It was like "rock, paper, scissors" except everyone lost.

After thirty minutes of driving in traffic, we exited the freeway onto a small street that didn't have a street sign. We followed the suspicious directions that our friend—who was DJing the party—gave to us. After a few twists and turns through a labyrinth of nothingness, we ended up on a quiet cul-de-sac.

"Is this it?" I asked.

"This is where the directions end," Spoons replied, sipping out of a plastic vodka bottle with a brand that was popular amongst the homeless population.

The street was empty. A few cars were scattered but not enough to indicate a party. The street lights were few and far between, leaving the dead end nearly pitch black. Unlike L.A., the stars shone brightly in the inland sky. We continued drinking our respective bottles of booze as we sat idly in the car.

"Whoa, dude, look at that girl," Spoons pointed.

"Wow, she's stunning."

Across the street, a blonde, curly-haired woman—a good four inches shorter than me—emerged from the darkness of the street. Her high heels clacked as she sauntered by. She rounded a corner disappearing behind a house.

"You think that's where it's at?" Spoons asked.

"Doesn't look like there are other options," I suggested.

I tapped my bottle of whiskey against his bottle of vodka. We carried them with us as we rounded the corner behind the house. A rickety gate stood before us. Beyond the gate was a spacious backyard filled with people. We paid the cover charge and crossed into our first party in the I.E.

A crowded dance floor bounced below the DJ booth. A makeshift bar loomed on the opposite end. Next to it was a small area where people were inflating balloons. Butch lesbians, tall women, and feminine guys roamed the party. The cold inland wind blew hard, forcing me to take frequent swigs of whiskey to stay warm.

"The I.E. is pretty lit," I said.

"We should come out here more often!" Spoons replied.

A giant woman glided past us. Her fiery red hair flowed in the autumn wind. Her broad shoulders shimmied from side to side. A small tattoo peeked from beneath the sleeve of her dress. Her muscular calves flexed with every step of her heels. Her height was so incredible, even Spoons had to look up to see her face.

"Geez," Spoons whispered to himself. His eyes bulged out of his face.

I had watched Spoons have sex with enough women to know exactly what his type was. In fact, I lost my female virginity with Spoons in a threesome. We didn't touch each other in any way—because we were friends and I had a higher standard—but we both shared a willing girl he once dated. Him and I split the expense of a motel room like the classy fellows that we were. He showed me how to go down on her, among other things. We were bonded as best friends ever since.

"Go talk to her," I urged.

"No, I can't. She's way too pretty. Besides, I just want to hang with you tonight. Boys' night out, remember?" He said, putting his arm around me.

We bought a few drinks after finishing the bottles of alcohol we brought in. We danced to the hip-hop music despite Spoons having zero rhythm, wearing jeans from the 90s, and sporting those dad shoes that had the letter "N" on them.

Watching him dance was like watching Wreck-It Ralph trying to play Hopscotch. It was a sight you couldn't take your eyes off of, and I wasn't the only one at the party that agreed. Spoons captivated everyone's attention. He stole the spotlight on the dance floor. I stood against a wall sipping my whiskey faster than I wanted to, partially because of the cold weather, but also because I drank faster when I was alone.

Soon enough, the DJ transitioned to a song too fast for my uncoordinated friend. He joined me in the designated pissing corner of the backyard that was only hidden by a shrub.

"Spoons, you're my best friend, man!" I slurred while pissing.

"No, dude. You're my best friend," he answered, with his own stream of urination exiting his body.

"Dude, I love you."

"Man. I. Love. You."

We shook our respective genitals and followed the drunk "I Love You Man" ritual with a customary hug.

We made our way back to the DJ area. While we stood, the fiery-haired woman glided through the party once more. Only this time, she landed in front of us. We marveled at the beauty.

"I liked your dancing," she said to Spoons, with a bass in her voice deeper than the music. She must have been just as delusional as him.

"Thanks," Spoons replied.

"Do you want to dance with me?" She asked.

I could hear Spoons' heart pounding. I could feel the floor shake beneath his quivering legs. I could even see the drool dribbling down his beard.

"I'd love to, but I don't want to leave my friend," he replied.

"Are you stupid?" I blurted. "For the love of god, go dance, you gaping rectum!"

"But what about—"

I shoved the big man toward the even bigger woman. What kind of best friend would I have been if I let him pass up an opportunity like that? There would be plenty of other times to have a boys' night, but this woman was a rare gem.

Spoons walked with her toward the dance floor, glancing back at me. Although I encouraged him, the moment felt like the end of Superbad where they went their separate ways on the escalator; or like Ricky Bobby and Cal Naughton Jr. breaking up shake 'n' bake.

I stood against the wall with the one friend that would never leave me: Jack Daniels.

After cycling through some songs, the DJ stepped away from her equipment.

"I'm surprised you guys ended up coming," she said to me.

"Why?" I asked. "You always invite us to these house parties, and we wondered why we never come out to the Inland Empire."

"Yeah, T-parties aren't really everyone's thing."

"T-party? What's a T-party?"

"Are you serious?" She laughed. "Look around."

With great effort, I tried to focus on looking at the party in front of me. It looked the same as when we entered except much more blurry: butch lesbians, tall women in dresses, and feminine guys.

"It's a tranny party," the DJ informed me.

"Oh," I replied.

She couldn't stop laughing at how oblivious I was.

Before drag queens broke through to the mainstream— long before Rupaul's Drag Race—not a lot of men openly wore dresses to clubs. Not even the gay clubs. These men in dresses were also not always performers. Some of them were just guys that enjoyed wearing women's clothing and being called "trannies". Our friend was apparently a revered DJ at these types of parties.

She returned to her booth, leaving me to process the T-party by myself. I stood awkwardly when a deep, angelic voice fluttered toward me.

"Do you want some?"

I turned to see the curly-haired blonde that Spoons and I saw when we first pulled up to the house. She was even more mesmerizing up close—her overly highlighted cheeks glistened beneath the moonlight, her dark eyes matched her deep purple lips. I wondered why this girl was so dressed up for a house party until I remembered what the DJ had said. The beautiful blonde was definitely a tranny.

"Some what?" I choked out.

She was sucking on a halfway deflated balloon with an imprint of "Happy 1st Birthday" on it. She inhaled its contents. Her eyes rolled to the back of her head. A devious smile spread across her face.

"Nos." She giggled.

"Sure," I replied, trying to avoid looking foolish for not knowing what Nos was. It was clearly some sort of drug, but I had never seen anyone do a drug that came out of a balloon. Except heroin but that was only in the movies.

She handed me what was left of the balloon. I inhaled the rest of the contents trapped within the first-birthday paraphernalia. A rush of dizzying euphoria raced to my brain feeling like an air pocket in a tub of water that exploded at the surface. Maybe it was my brain cells dying or an inhalation of happiness. I couldn't think straight either way. I giggled with the blonde.

Apparently, Nos was what people called nitrous oxide or, more commonly known as, laughing gas. The tank next to the bar was not just to inflate balloons for a party, but was an anesthetic drug they were selling through party favors.

The drug took me to an entirely new level of intoxication that I had never felt before. Actually, I couldn't feel anything. My vision was hazy and full of clouds but not the dark gray kind. Instead, it was euphoric, fluffy clouds that left me feeling weightless. It was like I was gliding through the early morning fog on Venice Beach. Only I wasn't at a beach paradise. I was at a T-party in the Inland Empire.

My body kept feeling like it was traveling through a dense fog until a bright light shined through. The clouds dispersed as the light got brighter. The euphoria dissipated with the fog, and I found myself blinded by the light glaring off a gun.

I was in a bedroom with a crib in the corner. Next to me was the blonde tranny—our hands interlaced together. I had the taste of wax on my lips. Her dark lipstick was smeared on her face. In front of us was a bed with an ungodly amount of meth piled in large plastic bags. On the other side of the mountain, was two large men and a rugged lesbian gripping a gun.

"What. The. Fuck," I whispered under my breath.

"What did you say?" The gun-wielding lesbo demanded.

I thought life-threatening situations were supposed to sober people up instantly. I thought death trumped any kind of intoxication. I thought if a woman with tattooed eyebrows was the Grim Reaper, my body would naturally revert to sobriety. I could not have been more wrong as I struggled to figure out how I got into that situation and, more importantly, how I was going to get out.

"So you got money or you wasting my time?" The lesbian growled.

I could feel my palms sweating while I held onto the tranny's hand. The light of the room was a stark contrast to the darkness outside. I could hear the DJ's set continue in the backyard. My eyes darted from the gun to the meth and back again. While most teenagers were deciding who they would ask to the Homecoming dance, I found myself wondering if I had enough cash on me to buy drugs just so the tweaked out lesbian didn't put a bullet through my body.

The music outside came to a screeching halt. It was replaced by the sound of yelling and glass shattering. The lesbian and two men ran out of the room toward the backyard. I followed them as quickly as humanly possible, towing the tranny with me.

A massive brawl was in full effect in the backyard. Wigs were not being snatched, nails were not digging into skin, and nobody was trash talking. Nobody worried about their eyebrows being smeared or their dresses being ruffled. Instead, there were fists being thrown and faces getting cracked.

The DJ shot a blast of pepper spray into the center of the action. A cloud rose like an A-bomb. Everyone dispersed trying to shield their eyes and cover their mouths. Like a true gentleman, I released the hand of the tranny to cover my own face. She couldn't stop coughing. Neither could the lesbian drug dealer or anyone else. I took the opportunity to make my exit. I stumbled around trying to get through the vortex of pepper spray and false eyelashes. Finally, I found the gate and faltered my way onto the street.

I escaped, staggering into Spoons by his car.

"Where the hell have you been?!" I yelled.

"What's happening in there?" He replied.

"We need to get out of here!" I struggled trying to open the passenger door.

"You're driving us back, remember?"

"I'm drunk!" I shouted.

"I'm drunker!" He shouted back.

The tranny rumble began spilling into the street.

"Fine!" Spoons admitted defeat, jumping behind the wheel. I got into the passenger side. The car skidded away from the T-party.

"I leave to fuck the redhead for five minutes and you get caught up in chaos?" Spoons reprimanded.

"You were having sex in the house while I was in a room full of meth?!" I shouted back.

"No, we had sex on the school playground down the street. Wait, you did meth?!"

"No, the lesbian with the gun just demanded I buy a Costco amount of it."

"Oh."

Spoons slammed on the brakes of the car, nearly causing me to eject the whiskey that was swishing in my stomach. He didn't see the red light at the intersection until the last second.

"I shouldn't be driving."

"No shit," I agreed.

We sat at the intersection when two police cars pulled up on either side of us with a third behind our car.

"Holy balls," I whispered.

"Just be cool," Spoons warned.

The light turned green. He casually drove ahead with the police cars all around us. With a labored focus, Spoons kept his wandering eyes on the road.

"I can't drive all the way home right now," he admitted.

"There's no way I can drive. Didn't you say Stephanie lives

around here?"

Spoons made a right turn with great effort. The police cars continued on their way. We exhaled sighs of relief.

"Yeah, they better keep driving!" Spoons yelled.

"Better not mess with us!" I joined in. "But, we should probably still go to Stephanie's to sober up."

"Fine," Spoons said, although he knew I was right.

After a few turns down dark streets, we pulled up to an uninviting apartment building. It looked more like a motel with no lobby or hallways. The unit doors opened to the outside. We climbed a flight of stairs to the second story, entering an apartment that looked like it should have been featured on an episode of Hoarders.

I caught a glimpse of Stephanie just before she took Spoons into her room, leaving me on the couch next to her gay brother and a very unfortunate looking female roommate. I pretended to watch T.V. with them, but all I could focus on was the stench of cat piss and microwave burritos. The sight, smell, and overall activity of that night was making me sick.

I couldn't let myself puke, though, because there was another gay guy in the room. I didn't want to be cock-blocked by my own vomit. I was annoyed that there was some accuracy to the idea of two guys having to be attracted to each other just because they were gay. At least, that's what happened at the end of the night when there was no other option. Apparently, nobody told the gay guy that that's how it was supposed to work, because he did not seem interested in the slightest. Or maybe nobody told the unfortunate looking roommate, because she kept babbling away about whatever was playing on the T.V.

I kept staring at the guy like he was my prey. It may have been the chaos of the party that had my adrenaline piqued or the opportunity to hook up with a beautiful tranny that literally slipped though my fingers. No matter the reason, I could feel my naughty zone pumping with blood and ready to go. But the ugly roommate insisted on talking and being ugly and ruining the night for the two gay guys in the room that desperately wanted to hook up.

"Can you just go to your room already?" I blurted out, very much to the girl's surprise.

"Um, what?" The uggo asked.

"I know it's your apartment and I'm a stranger, but can you just stop talking and go to bed? I just want to fuck your friend. Don't worry, nothing raw."

She looked at the gay guy then back at me before finally getting off the couch she had sunken into and headed toward her room.

"Finally," I groaned when her door closed. I scooted closer to the guy.

"Um, yeah, I'm going to go now. It was nice meeting you," he said politely, getting off the couch. He was out the door before my brain could even put together a response.

I sat on the couch alone staring at the T.V. I let my head rest on a stained pillow. I picked up someone's bag of half-eaten M&Ms. I tossed a few red ones in my mouth and let the sound of Spoons having sex lull me into unconsciousness.

I was shaken awake what felt like only minutes later.

"We got to go," Spoons urged. "Like now."

"Where are we? What did you do?"

"I may or may not have flooded her toilet. Let's go!"

The sun was rising behind us as Spoons drove through the empty streets of the Inland Empire. The desert air was cool and crisp but wouldn't be for long. I was far from sober and the way Spoons swerved proved that he was too. We sat in silence for the entire drive back home.

He pulled up to my parents' driveway. I fell out of the car. "Um…"

"Let's never party east of here again," Spoons said.

"Deal."

HIV

Why were there tiny bumps on the ceiling? Why wasn't it flat like the walls? It seemed like a lot of effort someone had to put in to create a part of an apartment that was seldom focused on. I wondered if it was an aesthetic or if there was a practical reason.

It was dark in the room, but the halo of Santa Monica's light pollution was enough to allow me to concentrate on the details of the ceiling. I tried to count all the bumps that loomed above. One, two, three…

My head laid back on a pillow that wasn't mine. In a bed that felt too soft and expensive to be mine. In an apartment that was definitely not mine. Everything smelled fresh, especially the linen, which made it feel like that moment was premeditated. It was probably a comfortable bed to sleep in, but I wouldn't have known. It was not a time for sleep, even though I wished it was.

My head kept slightly banging against the wooden headboard as I kept counting the ceiling bumps. One hundred thirty-four, one hundred thirty-five. I wasn't sure whose bed it was, but I assumed it belonged to the person that I was having sex with. He was sweating profusely, nearly out of breath. It looked like he was putting a great effort into his conquest of my sixteen-year-old body. One hundred fifty-eight…

I didn't want to be in that soft bed. I didn't want to be in that fancy apartment. I didn't want to be having sex. But I was. A person whose name I didn't even know was taking control of my body. All I could do was hope it would be over soon. Two hundred sixty-three. My face cringed every time he tried to kiss me. Two hundred sixty-four. The high ceiling felt like it was getting further and further away, like my innocence.

Two hundred sixty-five.

The sweaty man orgasmed with great pride, as if he did an honorable service. His body slumped beside me letting his arm drape across my naked body. Two hundred sixty-six. It was finally over and not a ceiling bump too soon. A deep snore resonated from the stranger. I slipped away from his heavy arm and off the bed. I put my pants back on, relieved to cover my body.

I shut the front door quietly, leaving my childhood behind. It wasn't the first time I had sex, but it was definitely the first time I had unwanted sex. It was the first time I hoped it would end. It was the first time I wanted to run out of a room and never look back.

I didn't tell him 'no'. I didn't try to fight him off. I wasn't physically forced. Instead, I learned that when a man invited you over to watch movies, it strictly meant sex. My rose-colored glasses were stomped and shattered, leaving me staring face-to-face with the ugliness of reality. I was only a kid, but I had become a person capable of putting themselves in desecrating situations.

*   *   *

"Holy tits, this place is way different during the day!" I shouted, stunned at the sight of Boystown.

Ash and I were strolling around WeHo toward the park. We had just finished eating at Fiesta Cantina—which I had learned sold food and not just ridiculous-sized margaritas. The contrast of Boystown between day and night was, well, day and night. There were casually dressed people having lunch at various high-end places. Straight couples hung out with their young children. People in business suits shouted on their cellphones.

"Do these people even know what happens here at night?" I asked Ash. "I've seen multiple people puke in that very spot where that kid is standing."

"I got a BJ down that alley once." Ash pointed toward a straight couple with a puppy.

We strolled around, passing all the bars that pretended to be dining establishments during the day. The smell of deep-fried food wafted through the air. As we continued, we passed the free HIV-testing truck that was often parked in the area at night.

"WeHo, where you can devour unseasoned tacos and get tested at the same time," Ash said. "You want to get tested?"

"I'm having a good day," I replied. "I don't want to ruin it by finding out I'm positive or something. Besides, I'm already waiting for my results from the clinic in Hollywood. Should be getting them today or tomorrow."

"I don't think HIV would ruin your day," Ash responded.

"Are you kidding? It would ruin my life! But you're more than welcome to get tested."

"I can already tell you the results would come back positive," he said lightheartedly.

"Wait, what? Are you serious? You have HIV?" I whispered.

"Yes ma'am. I'm positive," he replied in a normal tone of voice.

"How? Are you dying? Do you still have sex? Are you on medicine? Sorry. That's probably rude to ask. I've never met someone positive." I whispered the last part.

"I'm sure you have. People just don't really talk about it. It's still pretty stigmatized and a lot of people are ignorant to what it actually means." He looked me up and down.

"Sorry."

"I'm undetectable," he explained. He rolled his eyes off of my look. "Which means I can't transfer it."

"Man, life would suck if I was positive," I contemplated. "Aw, I didn't mean it like that. It's just—I might be positive."

It was the first time I admitted out loud that my status was in question. I wasn't sure if I felt better after I said it. Ash was being so open with me that it made me comfortable enough to reciprocate.

"Are you okay?" He asked.

"I'm not sure. I guess I'm pretty scared, to be honest. You being so calm about it makes me unsure how to feel."

"There's treatment and medicine now. The only part of HIV that hasn't progressed is the judgment people have toward it."

Although Ash was being open about his status, there was worry behind his words. It was as if he wasn't sure how I was going to react to him. He seemed the tiniest bit concerned that I would reject him. It was as if he had had that conversation with someone before with a different outcome.

*   *   *

A year after I had the unwanted sex in the luxury apartment, I graduated from High School. I was seventeen, had my own car, and was excited to download an app called Grindr. My part-time job at Taco Bell didn't occupy nearly enough hours of my life. I had nothing but time and a glorified sex app on my hands. So I did what any gay teenager would do in that situation.

One afternoon, I would drive to Burbank to sleep with a guy that managed a tanning salon but also had a monstrous penis. The next day, I would drive to Koreatown to sleep with the creepy guy that had an obsession with home security. While we were having sex, I stretched out my arm and accidentally knocked a couple guns out from beneath his pillow.

On another day, I would drive to my regular's house. Well, his parents' house. He was ten years older than me—a High School teacher that always commented on how I looked like I could be one of his students. We'd have sex while Family Guy played in the background. His statue of the Virgin Mary loomed above his dresser, judging us. Once we were done doing the dirty, I would have to jump out of his window because he didn't want his parents to see an underage boy leaving his bedroom.

Grindr was the greatest thing ever invented to my undeveloped mind. I had spent my entire life feeling alone. I felt like I was the only gay person in the world. Then, suddenly, I had access to guys in my vicinity. My hormones were elated.

"The last guy I had sex with was so weird," I told Spoons and our mutual friend, Liam. "When he orgasmed, he would shout 'I'm going to blast! I'm going to blast!' I felt like I was fucking Buzz Lightyear."

We were sitting in Liam's studio apartment. He was the kind of friend that nobody liked, but he was the only one with their own apartment, so we kept him around.

"I think it's kicking in," Spoons boasted with serenity. He had just taken a couple painkillers and washed them down with spiced rum. I had already been feeling the half pill he tossed me, but that was because I was a hundred fifty pounds lighter than him.

"Here, have some more alcohol," Liam encouraged. He poured us two shots even though Spoons was already laying facedown on the floor. Of course, I couldn't let the alcohol go to waste so I drank them both.

"Where's yours?" I asked Liam.

"I've had enough," he replied. Despite being a few years older than me and twice my size, he had a much lower tolerance.

"I got to go," Spoons said, muffled by the carpet.

"I don't think you're in any shape to drive," I said.

"No, no. I'm not driving. I texted one of my girls to pick me up."

"Which one this time?" I asked.

"The big, white one with the massive breasts," Spoons answered.

Liam and I exchanged a look. "Yeah, that doesn't narrow it down."

A knock echoed from the door. Liam opened it to reveal a Spoons girl. She lived up to the mold of all the other girls he slept with. With maximum effort, she managed to walk his carcass out of the apartment.

I wasn't expecting Spoons to leave so early. I was far too intoxicated to drive myself home. I was stuck in Liam's apartment until I could sober up. I really didn't want to be there, but I didn't have much of a choice. The painkiller was doing its job, and the rum was encouraging it.

"I'm just going to hang a bit to sober up," I said, curling up on the end of the bed.

"You can spend the night," Liam replied.

"No, it's cool. I just need a minute."

I rested my head against a pillow. I felt Liam lay down behind me. He slowly put his arm around my body. Although I wasn't attracted to him in the least, it felt kind of nice to be held. Besides, I had cuddled with plenty of my friends before.

Then, I felt his hand wander around my hip. Despite my body being numb, I could feel my pants being removed. Then a piece of flesh grazed my skin. My eyes shot open. I knew what was happening, but I didn't stop him. I didn't say 'no', and I didn't push him away. But I was fully aware that I didn't want what was about to happen.

I wanted to run out of the apartment, but I didn't force myself up. Instead, I passively laid there allowing someone I considered a friend to take advantage of a situation.

"I feel sober," I lied. "I'm going to go."

"You should stay. We can get breakfast in the morning," he replied.

I carried my legs toward the door. The painkiller hadn't worn off, but I felt much safer on my own than in that apartment.

I avoided Liam's text messages after that day. A conditioned discomfort consumed my body every time I saw him when we hung out with our circle of friends. It made me even more sick to know that he didn't have any idea how miserable I felt.

I took a hiatus from Grindr. I tried to meet people the

old-fashioned way—in person. However, for any queer person, it was a dangerous venture to try to meet someone. It was difficult to tell if someone was gay or straight, closeted or out. Even if I met someone that was gay, there was no way to tell if they accepted it or if their self-hatred projected on the entire community. Simply trying to talk to someone created an anxiety unparalleled in the straight world. No matter how sleazy dating apps could have been, they at least reassured me that I wasn't the only queer person in the world.

I returned from my brief Grindr hiatus to meet Carlos. We had sex regularly but kept it completely professional. We never hung out outside of his bed, and I never lingered after the deed was done. We took all precautions to never actually get to know each other.

It was refreshing to meet someone who lived in a house that wasn't their parents'. I didn't have to crawl through his window to get in. I was encouraged to use the front door like a human. He didn't have guns underneath his pillows, and he didn't have Virgin Mary statues judging us. He seemed like a pretty decent person and, at that point, that's all I could hope for.

On a cold night around the holidays, I was struck with a spout of insomnia caused by a spontaneous depression. It may have been the cold weather, or that time of the year that made me feel particularly lonely. Whatever the reason, I was scared to be alone with my own thoughts.

"Hey, you doing anything?" I asked Carlos over the phone.

"Just watching T.V." He replied.

"I'm not feeling great. Is it cool if I come by? Just to lay down and watch a movie or something. I'm not down for sex tonight."

"Yeah. That actually sounds nice."

I got in my car and headed toward Carlos' house. I kept the windows down to feel the cool wind of the late night. Blink-182's "I Miss You" was playing on my iPod because, for some reason, listening to sad songs when I was already depressed made me feel better—like sweating out a cold. I pulled up to the dark house and joined Carlos in his room.

I glanced around noticing the contents of his bedroom for the first time. He had a fish tank with neon rocks on the bottom. Batman movie posters hung on the walls. His closet didn't have doors; it showed off his array of clothing that was mostly button-up shirts. We laid down together on his bed, watching Netflix. He put on an animated movie and put his arm around me.

I could feel the chemicals in my brain rebalancing with a small rush of endorphins. It was comforting to not be alone. I could feel myself finally drifting toward a euphoric sleep. Then I felt Carlos' hand reach into my pants. He pushed his body against mine. Then, he pulled my basketball shorts down followed by my Calvin Kleins.

"I'm not down for sex tonight," I reminded him.

"That's fine," he assured me.

He continued fondling me for a bit, then he pushed himself against my body.

"Ow," I cringed. "Not tonight. I told you I don't feel good."

My heart was pounding from the abrupt pain he caused. He stopped leaning into me. He draped his arm back around my body. My adrenaline subsided, and I was able to drift back to sleep until Carlos pressed his body against mine once again.

He shoved himself into me. My body jerked forward in excruciating pain, but his arm prevented me from jumping too far.

"Stop," I told him. "It hurts."

"It's okay," he whispered in my ear as he started thrusting, pushing further into me. "It's okay. I'll be fast."

I reached behind me, putting my hand on his hip to try to push him away. I winced in pain with every dry thrust. I couldn't count the bumps on the ceiling to distract myself. I couldn't count down the seconds until it was over. I couldn't think about anything other than the pain that was surging through my body and the betrayal that ravaged my mind.

I needed someone that night. I needed to not be alone. I

didn't have a lot of gay friends, so I went to a place where I thought I might be able to connect with someone. It was naïve of me to think I could fill my emotional emptiness with the company of a stranger, just because they were part of the LGBT+ community.

He continued. I was terrified of moving. Part of me thought that maybe I deserved it for some reason. Another part of me thought it was a small price to pay for someone else's satisfaction. My thoughts were cut short by the pain of each jab into my body. He finished.

We laid there. His arm still gripped me. I stared out the window, afraid to blink my eyes. I wanted to run out of that room as quickly as I could but, for some reason, I didn't want to make it seem like I was uncomfortable. I continued to lay in the bed for a few more minutes. Finally, I got up rushing to put my shorts and shoes back on.

Carlos kissed me as I was about to leave. I was repulsed. I didn't wait for him to walk me to the door. I let myself out of his room and out of the house.

I bounded to my car and drove away as quickly as possible. I could feel tears welling up in my eyes, but I didn't let them fall. I didn't allow my mind to wrap around what just transpired. I didn't register the emotion I felt. Instead, I cocooned my mind—shielding it from an imminent breakdown.

I called Milo.

"Sorry to wake you. Can I come by for a second?"

Milo was one of my few friends that was always there for me when I needed him. Without hesitation, he invited me over.

I pulled up to his house minutes later. Milo was in his pajamas, shivering in the driveway waiting for me. I raced toward his outstretched arms. Once I felt the warm embrace of my friend, my emotions became unhinged; I couldn't keep my mind numb any longer.

Tears streamed my face. I fell to the ground with Milo holding me tightly. His shirt was soaked with my tears. I never wanted to leave the comfort of his arms. He didn't ask a single question. He gave me the opportunity to fall apart because he was there to hold me together.

＊　　　＊　　　＊

"This place is actually really nice," Ash said, as we strolled around the West Hollywood park.

The innocent laughter of children galavanting around the jungle gym drifted around us. Groups of guys were shuffling around the basketball courts. Casual readers spent the afternoon resting on the blades of grass.

"Who would have guessed this park was used for activities other than late-night BJ's after getting kicked out of The Abbey," I said.

"That was really specific."

We found a comfortable spot in the luscious grass. We basked beneath the sun. It was the first time I had absorbed vitamin D at the park that wasn't a euphemism.

"You look like you're stuck in your head," Ash noted.

"Yeah… I don't know. Maybe there are worse things than being HIV positive."

"You could be Republican." Ash laughed.

"I'd rather have the disease," I replied, not sure if I was joking. "You seem so happy. I thought being positive would depress a person."

"I'm not going to lie, some days are worse than others. Like when people say I'm 'not clean' or whatever—ignorance can be annoying."

"Sorry I was ignorant."

"At least you asked questions instead of just dropping me from your life," Ash said.

"That was really specific."

The sun began to set. We could feel the atmosphere of WeHo transitioning into the chaotic late-night world of Boystown. The families left the park and the distant sound of Ariana Grande boomed from the surrounding clubs. Happy Hour had turned into the pre-game. The pre-game was now turning into game time.

I decided to walk home while Ash grabbed himself a Lyft.

I was two miles away from my apartment, but I appreciated the time of solidarity. Thoughts kept flooding my mind. All the memories of the times I had sex without a condom flashed before me. I cursed myself at how such a simple, easy task could have prevented the predicament I was in. I had no one else to blame but myself, and I was going to have to live with the consequences.

Ash was not defined by his status. He was simply a person that happened to be positive. There was no black cloud over his head. There was no sadness in his eyes. He didn't feel bad for himself. He just lived his life like any other person would.

I checked my phone repeatedly on my way home, hoping the clinic had sent me an email. I sauntered into my apartment and slumped onto my bed. My eyes were getting heavy despite how early it was. Then my phone vibrated. I reached over for the illuminated screen to see a text from Ash:

Thanks for not judging.

I smiled. He was appreciative, but had no reason to thank me. We were friends, and it didn't matter if he was positive or negative. I was just happy he felt comfortable enough to share something so personal with me. I closed the text message, then opened my email again. After refreshing, an email from the Los Angeles LGBT Clinic popped up.

This was it.

I was about to find out if my life was going to change forever.

The email opened.

My eyes scanned the message. Chlamydia: negative. Syphilis: negative. HIV: negative.

I waited for a breath of relief to escape my body but it never did. I waited for my legs to hoist me into the air in celebration but they never did. I waited for a grin to reach my ears, but that didn't happen either. I was relieved knowing that my status was no longer a question mark. The results, however, did nothing for my mind. HIV was no longer something that I was afraid of.

I rested my phone beneath my pillow and laid my head back down. I closed my eyes thinking about how many of my other friends could have had HIV, but felt too afraid to talk to me about it. It disappointed me to think that I wasn't a person that they could come to.

I reached for my phone to text Ash back:

I'm always here if you need to talk.

PART III

SAINT PETER D'VIL

I was in a battle of wits with Grayson at his bar. "Battle of wits" meaning a drinking match. Only it wasn't my usual whiskey drink of choice. Instead, it was the deliciously strange Italian liqueur known as Fernet. Since any drinking game followed house rules and Grayson was the owner of the bar, it was Fernet all night.

The buzz circulating my brain felt more like a high than a drunk. The various herbs and spices that comprised Fernet was a mixture that altered reality. Once used as medicine, Grayson swore that it could cure anything. If that was the case, then we had the two healthiest bodies on the planet after all we had consumed.

We took a shot.

"Good job, princess," Grayson bellowed with his English accent, before slamming the back of his hand—just the tips of his fingernails—into my crotch.

"Holy balls!" I keeled over. A surge of pain electrified my body worse than if he just punched me straight forward.

"Stop your whining."

I stepped outside to regain my breath and to get some

feeling back in my genitals. Once the pain dissipated, I was able to enjoy my buzz again.

"What happened?" A mousey voice asked me.

I turned around to see a guy with porcelain skin that looked even more pale compared to his vibrant green hair. The moonlight shined off his various piercings—three in his nose, snake bites, and gauges. He dressed in leather and had a white stone necklace in the shape of vampire fangs hanging from his neck. The smoke from his cigarette danced into the midnight sky. An enigmatic allure radiated from him.

"Oh, nothing," I answered.

"I'm Adrian," the enigma said.

"What are you doing here, Adrian?"

"What do you mean?"

"You don't look like the typical people in WeHo," I replied.

"I can say the same about you. Guess there aren't that many places for tatted up fags in leather like us." He smirked. "Want to grab a drink?"

We went back into the bar where I continued matching shots with Grayson. We included Adrian as a special guest, but the poor guy turned out to be a lightweight. Suddenly, he was more intoxicated than me. He excused himself to use the restroom.

"Where'd you find this one?" Grayson asked me.

"He's not like all the other ones."

He rolled his eyes.

"I swear! I really like him. Pretty sure I'm in love and going to marry him," I said for the eighth time that month.

When Adrian returned, the bar started filling up with the usual WeHo crowd. Like a siren's song, the pop music flowing through the speakers lured in the drunk people that listened to the whispers of vodka telling them they could dance. We got pushed to the side of the tiny bar.

"You like this kind of music?" Adrian asked.

"It's all right," I shrugged to the sound of Fifth Harmony. "I wish I didn't have to hear it at every gay bar, though."

"What do you usually listen to?"

"You know, like 70s and 80s punk music. Circle Jerks, Sex Pistols, Dead Kennedys, The Pixies," I told him.

"The Pixies?" Adrian asked. He pulled out a pair of earphones from his pocket and shuffled through his iPod. He handed me an earbud, and he took the other.

With your feet in the air and your head on the ground...

I was getting lost in his piercing green eyes as they glowed under the dim lights of the bar.

Try this trick and spin it, yeah...

Drinks spilled all around. People bumped into us. The bar was covered with skinny people trying to twerk.

Your head will collapse, but there's nothing in it...

My face moved closer to Adrian's. I knew there was a Top 40 song playing somewhere outside of the iPod, but all I could hear was The Pixies.

And you'll ask yourself... Where is my mind?

For the next few minutes, time didn't exist. There was no such thing as existence. There was only energy. The energy of the crowd was strong, but the energy in the sanctuary shared between the enigmatic boy and me was stronger. We were keeping each other safe from the world around us—the world that we didn't fit in—if only for just a moment.

"I want to show you something," Adrian said.

He led me down Santa Monica Boulevard through Boystown, passing muscled guys and straight girls. He pulled my hand. Our Doc Martens stomped across the rainbow painted street. Finally, he stopped in front of a building.

"Mickey's?" I asked.

He pointed at the banner strewn across the top of the building:

SAINT PETER'S WHORE HAUS.

The 'A' was stylized as a pentagram and the 'T's were upside down crosses.

"Whore Haus?"

Adrian smiled leading me in.

This wasn't the Mickey's that I had known. It was transformed into a completely different world: black jeans and T-shirts replaced button-ups; The Devil's Rejects played on the

T.V. instead of pop music videos; rather than jacked-up, muscly go-go dancers there were pale guys covered with tattoos. The people in the crowd ranged with styles from horror, to gothic, to hardcore, and even punk. And not the H&M-Marilyn-Manson-T-shirt-wearing "punk" but legitimate punks that had actually survived a mosh pit or two.

"How can this be Mickey's?" I asked Adrian. "Is this even a gay event? I didn't know there were gay people like us out there."

"This is Saint Peter D'vil's event." He pointed at his fang necklace. "He makes these to show us we're not alone." He spoke of Saint Peter as if he was some sort of savior.

We wandered around the venue, coming across a small stage where a drag queen was performing. He didn't dance. He didn't gyrate. He didn't death-drop or cartwheel. The queen in black lingerie held up a needle for the crowd to see. A melancholic song reverberated through the building. The queen took the needle, pressed it against his leg, and pierced through his skin. Drops of blood trickled down his leg to his leather combat boots. He took another needle and repeated the feat over and over again, each time with bigger needles, until his entire thigh was covered with metal.

This was a surreal dream come true for a queer kid that grew up attracted to punk music and horror. Often times I would have to choose between a venue that catered to a queer crowd and a venue that catered to a punk crowd. Although queers and punks had been nearly synonymous in history, I had never known an event in Los Angeles that combined both worlds.

"I want to meet Saint Peter," I told Adrian.

The lights rose in the venue and the music faded away.

"Maybe next time," he assured me.

*   *   *

I had lost Adrian's phone number shortly after we hung out, and it wasn't just an excuse to ghost him. Unlike everyone else I had ever connected with, I didn't intend to lose contact with him.

A few years passed. I had become fully integrated into the DTLA underground drag scene. Isadora was gaining more and more exposure from competing in the Wepa competition; Pinché and I were hanging out frequently; and the drag scene was exploding. Danny Lethal's fetish events were thriving in Los Angeles. The Boulet Brothers' shows were packed out the doors. Established gay bars like The Eagle and Akbar were becoming more popular than ever. Downtown L.A. had even started their own LGBT+ pride festival. It was a beautiful time to be queer outside of WeHo.

"You've got to blend that shit," Pinché said, referring to Isadora's cheek contour. "It's looking like a sideburn."

"I already blended it! It looks fine," Isadora replied, staring into my restroom mirror.

"Ok, girl…"

Isadora blended his contour as soon as Pinché returned to painting his own face. For as sassy and stubborn as Isadora was, he became a student anytime a seasoned queen offered their advice. Even if sometimes he was reluctant.

There were no textbooks detailing how to cake makeup onto eyebrows. There was no school that taught how to disguise oneself as a woman. And there was definitely no PowerPoint to explain how to tuck your genitals behind you.

My apartment floor was unrecognizable beneath the palettes of makeup. Fabric filled the living room. Glitter and perfume soaked the furniture.

"What the hell is this?" I asked, lifting a heart-shaped piece of mattress.

"That's my ass," Pinché answered.

Pinché was shirtless with his legs stuffed into nylons with panties over them. His face was already painted and his hair was tied back. He was mid-transformation into his drag persona and it was a frightening sight to see.

He grabbed the pieces of mattress and shoved them unceremoniously down the sides of his nylon. Like two chicken drumsticks, he aligned them onto the sides of his legs, creating the illusion of hips.

"Drag is so strange," I said, completely fascinated by the detail. "What song are you performing tonight?"

"It's a secret." Pinché smirked.

"Just tell me."

"It's something you might be familiar with."

"Is it Justin Bieber?" I asked, obnoxiously.

"Yes," Pinché replied, flatly.

We were getting ready to go to Whore Haus for what was going to be my first time since stumbling upon the event years prior. The monthly show was a much bigger staple in the underground drag community than I had realized, although it was held in WeHo. It was the one night that the Downtown crowd ventured to the west side, harmoniously fusing the two distinct queer communities into one.

"Is it usually busy?" I asked.

"Packed," Pinché replied.

"You'll be fine," Isadora chimed in. "You can hide in the corner like you usually do at crowded places."

"It's not my fault I get anxious when I'm around a mass of people. I hate those kinds of places," I said.

"You just hate people in general," Pinché replied.

He wasn't wrong.

"You can't bail," Isadora continued. "Everyone is going to be there. Even Tristan."

"Are you serious?" I shot him a look.

"Relax. He's changed. This time for real."

"Changed like the time he allegedly stopped drinking but ended up busting his face on the concrete? Then you spent the rest of the night coddling him and feeding him sympathy."

"Serious?" Pinché asked. "That happened?"

"Or like the time he got eighty-sixed from the bathhouse?" I asked.

"Oh my god. Is that even possible?"

"It's different now," Isadora argued. "He wants to support my drag."

"We'll see."

Pinché and Isadora completed their looks with wigs and nails. The final touches of their personas were being added.

Pinché threw on his heels, and Isadora laced up his thigh-highs. Then Pinché put a black fang necklace over his head.

"Where did you get that?" I asked.

"The necklace? Saint Peter D'vil makes these. He's like the godmother of the underground drag scene. You do know that Whore Haus is his event? I'll introduce you tonight."

I was intrigued not only because of Saint Peter being a figure in the community, but also because I recognized the same kind of fang necklace that the enigmatic boy wore years before.

The two queens and I loaded into Isadora's car. My apartment was covered with shredded fabric and glitter that would never fully be removed. That was just one of the consequences (or bonuses) of hanging out with queens. I didn't know if I was going to wake up the next morning to find eyelashes in my bed, heels hiding in the restroom, or synthetic hair matted in the corners of my room. One thing queens never left, however, was alcohol.

Whore Haus was packed! Pinché was not exaggerating when he warned how many queers were going to be under one roof. And on the patio. And overflowing into the street. We arrived early, but the go-go dancers' thongs were already bursting with dollar bills.

"Let's see if we can find Saint Peter," Pinché suggested. "Should be easy. He looks like a witch that's had too much tequila."

I didn't feel like that narrowed down the field of people. Everyone looked like they were either going to summon a demon, or they were a demon themselves.

Then a statuesque drag creature strode through the sea of people. Rammstein powered through the speakers like an entrance song for the ethereal being. He was so tall but so in control of his body that each step was a calculated bound. His straight, blonde wig swayed. His tight, red leather outfit clenched his thin frame. The familiar fang necklace dangled from his throat.

He exchanged hugs with Pinché and Isadora.

"Hey," the queen with an unexpectedly human voice said.

I choked out a meager, "Hi."

"This is Dakota D'vil," Pinché told me. "He's Saint Peter's drag daughter."

If this was Saint Peter's drag daughter, then I couldn't even imagine what kind of commanding presence the godmother of underground drag was going to carry.

"Hey, puta!" A familiar voice clawed through the air.

Tristan strutted up to us. Isadora put his arms around his best friend, smothering him in his breasts. "Aw, I missed you."

Isadora noticed me cringe.

"Be nice," he warned me.

Tristan did look different than my memories of him. He was holding only one drink, and it wasn't spilling over. His eyes weren't crossed and the bags beneath them disappeared. But I was still skeptical. I had seen this routine too often. It was only a matter of minutes before the alcohol hit him in a way that he would refuse to control. He would end up embarrassing Isadora. Tristan was like a ticking time bomb that could never be stopped.

"I have to put my bags backstage," Pinché announced.

"Hurry up," I told him, feeling overwhelmed with anxiety. "There's way too many people here."

"You can come with me."

"No, I can't do that. It's okay."

"Come on. It' just going to be a bunch of queens getting ready."

Whore Haus wasn't getting any less crowded, and I already could have used a minute away from it all. Pinché handed me a bag, and I helped him carry it to a flight of stairs blocked off by stanchions. We ducked beneath the barrier and headed to the second floor of Mickey's. He led me to a door that was nearly hidden. We entered, continuing up another set of narrow steps.

I was in uncharted territory. I was about to enter an area reserved for performers only. It was a forbidden zone for regular people like me. Drag queens were the celebrities in our little underground community; they had such a powerful presence that I felt unworthy of being back there.

Images of queens, each with their own vanity mirror, raced through my mind. The thought of them snapping their fingers to get their assistants to bring them Fiji Water filled my thoughts. I imagined Saint Peter would have his own dressing room with his name written in gold across the top.

When we reached the top of the stairs, the music of the club was replaced with the sound of urgent voices. We came to an opening that led to the backstage area. I stopped.

"I really shouldn't be back here," I protested again.

Pinché rolled his eyes as I reluctantly followed him.

The dressing room was not exactly as I expected. Bar supplies were stacked in corners, extra tables rested throughout the area, and cleaning products were prominent. The walls were like an attic—exposed wooden beams with thin boards.

In each corner of the room, there were people preparing for the night. One corner had go-go dancers adjusting their junk for maximum appeal. Drag queens huddled in another corner, cinching their wigs and changing their outfits. I didn't know where to look. I felt like some kind of pervert wandering around.

To avoid staring at wieners—whether tucked or in jockstraps—I looked over to see bright lights illuminating an open restroom. There were even more queens getting ready for the show. Everyone seemed cramped but made do with what they had.

I was still feeling star-struck. I looked up to those drag queens the same way people looked up to actors, musicians, or any other kind of entertainers. I was a fan. I was inspired by them. It was a surreal moment for me being back there.

"Can you help me with this?" Luna Lovecock handed me a brush. He pointed at his wig.

"Um, what?" I asked, nervously.

"Just brush it out."

"Like how?"

"It's a fucking brush and a wig."

The logic was there, but I was so intimidated I couldn't think straight. I brushed Ms. Lovecock's wig, unintentionally making it worse than it was.

"Show starts in ten," a tiny voice shouted from the other side of the room.

"Shit, Saint Peter is going to start," Pinché said.

"That was him?" I asked.

Pinché nodded. I peeked at the other side of the room trying to get a glimpse of the mythical queen, but the action in the area picked up. All I could see was go-go dancers and men in dresses scrambling around.

I elected to wait downstairs for the show to start. I took a detour to the restroom. I waited in line, then finally passed the attendant that stood holding a damp towel, staring at his phone. His job wasn't just to offer people a mint or Starburst after they pissed like most attendants, but also to make sure nobody was doing drugs or getting blowjobs in the stalls. Apparently, I was an exception.

I ducked into a stall and raked some Adderall onto the back of my phone. I refused to do key bumps because keys were filthy instruments. Instead, I rolled up a flimsy five-dollar bill and let the amphetamine tickle my brain. Although uppers were the last thing someone with anxiety should have been doing, it took me out of my mind long enough to fully enjoy the night.

"Welcome everybody to Whore Haus!" A small voice traveled beyond the restroom walls. "I'm your host, Saint Peter D'vil."

I wrapped up the rest of the drugs, spun around in a circle trying to find the exit to the stall, grabbed a Starburst, and dashed toward the stage. I tried to shove my way through the crowd that surrounded the performance area, but nobody would budge. The music kicked on and the first performance was beginning.

A creepy, melodic voice whispered through the speakers. Scarlett Moon staggered grotesquely onto the stage, carrying himself with crutches. He moved like the girl from The Ring coming out of the well. The eerie music crescendoed with the growls of Marilyn Manson. Scarlett tore away part of his outfit, revealing a face painted like a demon. His eyes were flushed completely white. That drag monster would have eaten the rest of WeHo's picturesque beauty queens.

I finally made it to the side of the stage where Isadora stood with Tristan. They had a comfortable spot underneath a struggling air-conditioning vent. To my surprise, Tristan was upright and still sipping the same drink he had earlier. Isadora had a smile on his face. He looked genuinely happy to have his best friend next to him.

I found a spot adjacent to the stage as Scarlett Moon finished his number. He collected his tips and returned backstage.

Then a collection of rapid guitar licks cut through the air followed by a familiar female voice. The sharp guitar notes electrified the room. The DJ played a song from my favorite band. The Sounds brought the audience to life. They were the band that I credited with helping me survive my teenage years. I had played them on loop during my most pivotal moments— the nights insomnia struck, the first time I kissed a guy, the mornings that depression wouldn't let me get out of bed.

I questioned if I was dreaming. I would have never believed I'd hear The Sounds at a queer club. I scanned the room to see if anyone else even knew the song. I was amazed to see everyone cheering and singing along in a moment my teenage self would have never believed possible.

Pinché Queen marched onto the stage, clacking his heels. His hairy, exposed chest stood proudly over his black tights. He strutted the runway, lip syncing to The Sounds with a mixture of deep emotion and simple fun. We had bonded over our mutual love of the band before, but this was unexpected. Pinché sported a short, blonde wig—not unlike the lead singer's—performing one of the most inspiring songs in my life.

Pinché made eye contact with me. He nodded and smiled. I was elated. I felt the purity of being a teenager discovering art for the first time again. Whore Haus was truly an underground world that welcomed anything that diverted from the mainstream.

Everyone scattered once the performances concluded. A

sweaty Pinché raced up to me.

"What did you think?" He asked.

"Was that performance for me?"

"Hell no," he replied with a smirk.

We made our way to the patio. There was a massive circle of people outside. All the various queens I had met and more were trying to get to whoever was in the center. I tried to peer through the horde of people to see what the commotion was about, but all I could see was a sea of black clothing.

"I think Saint Peter is over there," Pinché pointed to the crowd. "I want you to meet him." Pinché started blazing a path to the center of the circle.

"That's a lot of people," I said to nobody listening. I was feeling claustrophobic and my anxiety was rising again. I slipped away from Pinché and the growing crowd.

For the first time that night, there was nobody at the bar. I decided to take full advantage. I ordered a drink and savored the whiskey almost as much as I savored the moment away from the crowd of people.

Next to me, a tiny drag queen placed a massive boot on the platform beneath the bar to elevate himself toward the bartender.

"Shot of tequila," the small voice requested. The queen grabbed a napkin and carefully blotted his makeup-covered face. "Jesus, there's so many people here."

"Yeah, it's a bit much," I said.

"I mean, it's good my event is packed, but I just need to get away from people for a minute."

"Your event?" I asked.

"Yeah, Whore Haus."

"Are you—You're Saint Peter D'vil?" I stared at the drag queen that was barely taller than me even with boots on. His straight, black hair resembled Elvira's. His eyebrows were pointed and thin like a chola vampire.

"Yeah, I'm Peter." He shook my hand. "I like your shirt."

I looked down at my Blondie shirt. I couldn't help feeling bashful. This was the most talked about queen in the underground drag community. Everybody had mentioned Saint

Peter D'vil to me at one point or another. His reputation was so incredible that it didn't match the tiny, humble queen that stood next to me. I would have felt unworthy of speaking to him if it hadn't been for our mutual dislike of crowds.

"But how can you be a drag queen and be uncomfortable around so many people?" I asked.

"I have anxiety around this many people."

"I don't think I've ever met a queen that was avoiding attention. You're Saint Peter."

"Saint Peter loves the attention," the queen continued. "But I'm still Peter underneath all the drag. I'm still a shy person."

"Shy?!" I shouted. "How can a queen be shy?"

"Well, that's why I do drag. The character of Saint Peter lets me be the person that I want to be."

I had been putting drag queens on a pedestal. I saw them as such celebrities that it never occurred to me that they were still humans underneath the four inches of makeup. Saint Peter was an integral pat of the underground drag scene but, on a human level, him admitting his anxieties was relatable.

People started coming up to Saint Peter. A crowd began to form. He took the tequila shot.

"Well," he shrugged.

The crowd split us apart. I drifted to the opposite end of the venue. I watched people dancing beneath the strobe lights, the go-go dancers gyrating, and drag queens mingling. As the night was coming to an end, people began dispersing until there was only a handful left in the venue.

With your feet in the air and your head on the ground…

The Pixies made its way to the speakers. The fast-paced night was concluding. The dance floor became visible again— covered with debris and spilled liquor.

Try this trick and spin it, yeah…

I made my way toward the exit.

And you'll ask yourself…

I turned to look at the club once more. Out of the corner of my eye, a glimpse of bright green caught my attention. Just below the DJ booth was a beautiful guy with porcelain skin.

Piercings covered his face, accentuating his sharp features. Beneath his vibrant green hair was a smile.

Where is my mind?

PINCHÉ COCHINO

"You sure you don't have a pee fetish?" Pinché asked.

"Pretty sure. I mean, I've never tried it," I explained. "I wish I was into it. I piss like twenty times a day. It's such a waste. I wish I could get some sort of pleasure out of it."

"You pee that many times?"

"That's not the point."

The Lyft driver shifted in his seat.

My phone lit up with an incoming message.

"Ooh, booty call?" Pinché asked.

"Actually…"

It was Gabriel. After getting my test results back, I felt comfortable enough to hang out with him a few times.

I returned my phone to my pocket.

"You're not going to text him back?" Pinché asked.

"If I texted him back, it would break my streak of ghosting people. I'm not a quitter."

"No, but you're an asshole."

"You're not wrong."

Our driver was visibly uncomfortable. We were only his second group of passengers ever. If he could put up with our fetish-gay-sex-ghosting-people conversation in the middle of the afternoon, then he was going to be good at his job. He hurried delivering us to our destination. I jumped out of the car looking forward to a plunge in my passenger rating either from the content of our conversation or the overwhelming volume of Pinché's voice.

We gazed around at the buzzing WeHo street before turning into Trunks. After a few unnecessarily stiff drinks, we hopped to the next bar. Then the next. And the next. Until we conquered the majority of the bars in Boystown. As we shifted passed Rage, a gaggle of gay boys sauntered by us.

"Why're you making that face? It's even worse than your usual Resting Bitch Face," I said to Pinché.

"Just not used to WeHo anymore," Pinché replied, looking around. "It's so much different than Downtown."

"Of course it is. But the music isn't that bad here."

"It's not the music. It's the people here that make me uncomfortable. How everyone looks down on other people. The whole vibe is stuck up."

I had always felt comfortable enough in both WeHo and Downtown. I didn't feel like I fit one hundred percent in either one, but they both had enjoyable qualities despite being completely different.

"C'mon, let's go to The Abbey," I suggested.

Pinché glared at me as if I had just suggested we throw our feces into oncoming traffic.

"What's wrong with The Abbey?" I asked.

"Are you serious?"

I dragged the protesting Pinché to the most famous WeHo bar. I ordered us a couple mixers with a few drops of alcohol in each that the bartender insisted cost twenty-eight dollars. I reached over the unnecessary amount of jars that held exotic fruit garnishes to retrieve our drinks. I handed one to the Bear Queen as he continued scrutinizing the place with a look of disgust.

"You really hate it here that much?" I asked.

"Look at it. It's a straight bar."

I examined the massive venue. The go-go dancers were blond, white guys with sculpted bodies. The women dancers were just as blonde with fake breasts and tans. Groups of people sat at booths, finding it necessary to yell "woo!" between every sip of their drinks. A collection of people with zero rhythm covered the dance floor.

Pinché and I grabbed a couple more shots as well as drinks that were more destroying my bank account than my liver. We were getting increasingly wrecked to the point that we were very obviously the sloppiest people at The Abbey.

"No, you're too drunk," I slurred at Pinché in response to nothing.

"What?"

"Where are all the cute guys at?"

"Not at The Abbey, you trashy bitch," Pinché snorted.

"Stop, it's not that bad here!"

"This place caters to straight people. It's so non-offensive and vanilla because it doesn't want to be too gay to where it scares off the straights. It's a 'straight acting' bar."

"That's so offensive," I told him. "Any queer spot that acts like something else would be awful."

The words "straight acting" cut deeply. It was a label that self-hating gays used to make themselves feel better about being queer. What they meant by it was that they weren't the stereotypical gays. Instead of just breaking stereotypes by admitting they were gay and being themselves, they further alienated our community by pretending to be straight.

I was getting heated with Pinché. I was offended that he believed I'd want to hang out somewhere that was heterosexual behind a queer mask. Then a tall, blonde guy wearing flip-flops and boot-cut jeans brushed by with a group of cackling girls. "Let's request the 'Cha-Cha slide'," we overheard him say.

"Holy Jesus," I whispered to Pinché. "This is a fucking straight bar!"

"What did I tell you?!"

I reexamined the venue, noticing just how vanilla it was. It was full of straight women with their boyfriends. Gays wearing superhero T-shirts from Target roamed around, somehow feeling superior to the flamboyant queers. It finally made sense. The Abbey was the most famous gay bar in L.A. because there were far more heterosexuals than queers in it!

"Let's get out of here!" I shouted before downing my overpriced drink.

"Thank you!" Pinché replied, finishing his drink faster than me.

On the way out, I reached over the bar grabbing a pretentious dragon-fruit garnish. I tossed it in my mouth because no bar needed such exotic fruits in their drinks. I strutted out of the venue enlightened.

"Fuck The Abbey."

"Fuck The Abbey," I agreed.

Pinché and I were playing on the borderline of blacking out, like a game of Chicken with our consciousness. We hopped on the next bus east. Despite the usual array of bus people—the screaming homeless man that was probably right about government conspiracies, the middle-aged cholo with his pregnant teenage girlfriend, the tourists that had no idea how terrible L.A.'s public transportation system was—we were the ones looking worse for wear.

"Should we go to Downtown then?" I asked, ignoring the little voice in my head that told me when I should go home.

"I think you've had enough," Pinché answered. "Next time, we're going to Precinct."

"Deal. I love that place."

"I can't wait to perform there one day," Pinché said. "I feel like I'm not even on the Boulet Brothers' radar, but I swear I'll perform for them soon."

"Do it. Meatball and Pickle perform there all the time."

"Hell, even Rubella Spreads has performed there, and she's… Rubella."

The bus was transitioning from West Hollywood into Hollywood. We were only a few blocks away from our stop, but we had to prematurely exit the vehicle. My stomach was twisting with that afternoon's festivities.

We fell out of the bus. I stumbled over to the closest

bush, bracing myself for the memories that were about to pour out of my mouth. I dry heaved over and over again. My mouth was salivating with the tease of regurgitation. I gagged, but nothing came out.

"Well, are you going to puke or what?" Pinché demanded, impatiently waiting for my discomfort.

"I can't!" I shoved my fingers to the back of my throat for a little inspiration. I waited. Nothing.

"Here, let me try."

Pinché jammed his fingers into my mouth like the supportive friend that he was. The taste of his old nail polish tickling my throat was enough. The sludgy regurgitation of whiskey projected out of my mouth, splattering all over the street. I laughed at the disgusting display of friendship when a second round of vomit spiraled up. My laughter snorted it out of my nose with an incredible velocity. The burn from stomach acid corroding my nostrils was excruciating.

"Uh-oh," Pinché cried.

Watching my body malfunction made him gag. His body hunched over heaving. I knew what was coming, but I couldn't get out of the soak zone quick enough. Pinché expelled his stomach juices all over my arm.

"Pinché!" I yelled. His insides stung my skin.

Before I could say another word, the favor was returned. I projected another stream of puke back onto him.

"You bitch!" He cursed me, thinking I did it on purpose.

He fired the next round at me with a devious intention. This went back and forth for the rest of the way to my apartment until there was nothing left to expel from our stomachs. We were like the Yin and Yang of vomiting queers trapped in a repulsive cycle.

We finally reached my building, drenched in chunky stomach bile.

"I need to shower," I said, rushing into my room.

"Me first." Pinché raced into the restroom ahead of me.

I stood in the middle of my apartment, trying not to touch anything while I waited for the Bear Queen to finish showering. I could feel pieces of his breakfast drying my arm hairs together. The stench was making me uneasy. I couldn't wait any longer. I shoved my way into the restroom, threw my clothes into the trashcan, and jumped into the shower.

Pinché's naked body almost toppled over in shock. I nearly collapsed on top of him.

"What are you doing?!" He yelled.

I pushed him away from the hot water, trying to rinse the regret covering my body. We fought over trying to get under the spout. The shower ran black with all the whiskey. I felt nostalgic watching it swirl down the drain. I scraped the remnants of vomit out of my nose. Finally, the water ran clear.

"Do you mind if I pee?" Pinché asked.

"After all we've been through tonight, I really don't care if you piss in the shower."

I scooted away from the drain and turned around to give him some privacy, although we were way beyond invading each other's personal space. While I shivered from being away from the water, I felt an uncomfortable warmth dripping down my thigh. I turned back around to see Pinché's expressionless face. His eyes were like slits. His mouth ran straight across.

"What the hell?!" I screamed.

Pinché did not flinch as he launched a steady stream of pee onto my leg. His expression remained the same throughout the lengthy urination despite my protest.

"You said you didn't mind." Pinché finally broke his concentration.

"I didn't think you were asking if you could piss on me!"

We stared at each other.

"How did we get here?" He asked.

"I don't know. But, now I know for sure that I don't have a pee fetish."

DRAGULA PART I

Tap! Tap! Tap!

A raggedy homeless man knocked, leaving smudges on my freshly washed car window. I rolled it down half an inch, fearing an inevitable stench.

"Yes?"

"Got a dollar?" He asked, pressing his cracked lips to the opening of the window.

"No." I rolled it back up.

"How about ten?" He retorted as if we were trying to compromise a deal.

"No."

The greedy homeless man trudged away with his shopping cart duplex. It was rude of him to interrupt my game of Candy Crush, but I wasn't about to let a stranger ruin my good vibes. I swiped a few candies and managed to achieve a personal high score. I was having a good day despite the homeless man trying to break my concentration on the important things in life.

My car was resting on the side of a one-way street in Downtown. The sun was trying to murder me with ninety-degree heat. My air conditioning was blowing hope into my idle car. It was parked in one of the only free parking spots in DTLA. Actually, it was parked along a red curb, but if an ambulance or fire truck needed the spot, I would move. Probably.

Pinché texted:

Ready. Pull up close.

I started the car and drove fifteen minutes across two intersections. Midday in Downtown was the last place I wanted to be. The streets were full of commuters that were above taking public transportation and tourists that thought they were getting real Gucci bags in Santee Alley. Business people in stuffy suits littered the sidewalks trying to ignore all the hotdog stands that pumped the delicious smell of bacon-wrapped street meat into the atmosphere.

I pulled up to Precinct. At night, the door looked like a portal into a mystical land but, during the day, it looked like it led to nothing more than an electrical closet between two restaurants. Nonetheless, the door cracked open.

Pinché's fully painted face peeked out. The scorching sunlight reflected off a glazed substance that covered his face. He pulled his body out of the doorway and trotted as best he could in heels. Daytime drag made his chest seem hairier, tights seem tighter, and his outfit—that was comprised of thin straps—seem even skimpier.

The Bear Queen ran across the sidewalk, forcing people to do double-takes. The business people, the homeless, and the tiny abuelas selling hotdogs stared in awe. Finally, Pinché reached my car.

"Unlock the damn door!" He shouted.

"I'm trying!" I shouted back through laughter.

The lock clicked. The door swung open. The sweaty queen jumped into the passenger seat, slamming the door behind him.

"Bitch…" He whispered, winded. His wig was matted in clumps. A gooey substance stained his face and dripped down to the rest of his body. His false eyelashes were sideways almost completely covering his eyes.

"You smell sweet," I told him.

He stared.

"So," I continued. "How was it?"

"Oh, you know, despite the honey in my eyes, I had a good day."

"Cool."

A few weeks prior, Pinché found out that he was being recruited to be on the inaugural season of a new drag competition show called Dragula. Created by the Boulet Brothers, Dragula was going to be a fusion of Rupaul's Drag Race and Fear Factor—a drag show with stunts and grotesque challenges. Rather than being held at a bar in front of a live audience—like most competitions—this one was going to be filmed as a web series. That afternoon, Pinché was at Precinct for a promotional video shoot where he dumped copious amounts of honey all over himself.

Each contestant was scheduled at different intervals throughout the day for the shoot. They would enter one way and exit another as to not cross paths. The contestants were still a mystery to everyone, including each other.

"The competition is going to be perfect for me," Pinché said, as I raced to drive him home. The stench of honey was already staining the seats.

"Well, if they're looking for trash then yes, you're definitely the favorite."

"Think about it. I'm going to have the biggest platform I've ever had. I'm going to be on a show. This is really going to launch my career. Plus the cash prize for the winner—I could really use that."

Pinché was excited about how this venture was going to elevate his drag to the next level. He was going to have the opportunity to prove just how talented he was, against a group of other queens.

I was a big fan of Pinché and I was becoming an even closer friend. His style of no-holds-barred drag was so different from anyone else that I had seen. His entire aesthetic had a punk feel to it. In a society that didn't always praise his body type, the Bear Queen carried himself with an untouchable confidence. He owned body positivity and promoted it with an intense passion.

For someone that grew up feeling like a hopeless gay kid, Pinché expertly turned his helplessness into empowerment with his drag. He was an incredible inspiration to me. He had my full support, and we both looked forward to seeing where the Dragula show would take him, not just in his career, but also in his personal life.

*   *   *

Pinché and I were on our way to Palm Springs. He was booked to perform at a club called Toucan's Tiki Lounge, and he could have used a mini vacation before Dragula started filming episodes.

"You really doing that?" He asked me.

"Relax, mom," I shot back. I ripped the plastic seal off a miniature bottle of Patrón. I watched a police car drive past us before downing the bottle of tequila. "Don't judge me; I'm on vacation."

"Right."

We were on a journey like Thelma and Louise, except we weren't running from questionable decisions—we were running toward them. I had bags full of Adderall, small liquor bottles for the road, alcoholic-sized liquor bottles for later, and a few dollars left over for a gas station sandwich in the morning. The only thing on our gay agenda for the next couple of days was to make sure Pinché got to his gig on time and to make sure I didn't die. One would prove more difficult than the other.

"I have to piss," I announced. The tequila was already making its way through my body.

I exited the freeway into a roundabout and sputtered into the parking lot of the all-too-convenient Morongo Casino. We used the facilities and were on our way back toward the car when the bright lights of the casino called to me like a siren's song. I turned toward the ocean of opportunity.

"What are you doing? We should really be getting to Palm Springs," Pinché warned.

"Just one hand," I told him.

Gambling was one of my many, many, (many) vices. I went to Vegas almost once a month. The high of putting what little money I had on a table in hopes of winning something life changing was far superior to any high from alcohol, drugs, or even sex.

When I was six years old, my dad should have won a Father of the Year trophy for teaching me how to add by playing BlackJack. He'd flip over cards, making me count how many I had. Then I'd either 'hit' or 'stay' trying to get to twenty-one without going over. I was destined to be a gambler from that moment on.

I circled around Morongo searching for the right table. I had fifty dollars in my pocket for the trip, so I needed one of the low-roller tables. The five-dollar BlackJack table was already full with a line of people hoping to sit down. The only other table open was in the High Roller section—a foreign territory to me. The area was for people that casually bet hundred-dollar bills like putting quarters in an arcade game.

I sat at an empty BlackJack table straightening out my crumpled dollar bills. The dealer stared at me like I was some sort of cruel prank. We both knew I didn't belong at that table. But the dealer had nothing else to do and no choice. I bet my fifty dollars. The biggest gamble was going to be whether or not I'd have money to buy food over the next couple of days.

"Good luck," the dealer customarily said.

She flipped over a Queen with a six for me. Then revealed an Ace for herself.

"Of course," I whispered to myself. It was a less-than-ideal situation. My hands shook with anticipation. There was a lot of money at stake for someone who didn't have money.

"Can you hurry?" Pinché asked, unamused.

I motioned for another card. The dealer tossed me a two —only slightly giving me hope. Despite the air-conditioned oasis of the casino, I could feel droplet of sweat form.

"Ready?" The dealer asked perversely.

"Let's do it."

She flipped over her card—a five—and had to keep accepting cards. Finally, she busted.

"Yes!" I shouted.

The dealer paid me out. I stood up gathering the unimpressive amount of chips she handed me.

"That's all?" She asked with a smirk that was both alluring and offensive.

"I just bet all the money I brought," I replied.

"Are you serious?" Pinché asked.

"Gambling," I shrugged.

I cashed in my chips for an amount that was nearly all the money to my name. As we strode to the exit, I stopped.

"No more gambling. We have to go," Pinché whined.

"You down for a shot?" I pointed at the bar.

He didn't protest. I used my extra winnings on two grossly overpriced tequila shots. We clinked our glasses, savored the liquor, then returned to the car. We drove further into the desert with the sun directly overhead. We were still a few hours away from Pinché's show.

"Wait a second." I gazed around over the steering wheel. "This area doesn't look familiar."

"Did you get us lost?"

"Of course not," I replied.

"Should I Google directions?"

"No, no, it's cool. I know where we are."

"It says we're passed Palm Springs."

"I said not to Google directions!"

As it turned out, maybe taking shots while traveling over a hundred miles was not the wisest decision. We were miles passed the route to Palm Springs. If we continued a bit further, we would have hit Arizona.

"If we keep going this way, we'll end up in my hometown, and I definitely don't want that," Pinché warned.

"All right. Hang on."

I slowed the car down to a cool 70mph, yanked the

steering wheel to the left, and pulled a U-turn through a mound of dirt that separated the sides of the freeway. My tiny car buckled over the loose rocks. We landed on the opposite side of the freeway. I opened my eyes.

"There," I said triumphantly.

Pinché clung to the bar above the window, giving me the side-eye.

We finally arrived at the resort in one piece. We were the only car driving through the Palm Springs desert and the only one in the parking lot. We sauntered into the lobby, half expecting the place to be closed. We loitered by the front desk.

"You sure this is the right place?" Pinché asked.

"Pretty sure," I replied, even though I was the one that booked the room.

It was a very clean, well-manicured resort that we had no business being in. On the other side of the lobby windows were towering walls that kept the pool secluded.

"Do you think this is one of those clothing optional resorts?" I whispered.

Before Pinché could answer, a very attractive young guy— that may have had Down's Syndrome—came up from behind the desk.

"Checking in?" He asked.

"Yeah," Pinché answered for me. He nudged my arm to get me to stop staring at the attractive guy.

We left the lobby, immediately entering the pool area. The inviting water was a sparkling paradise. It was completely still with a single raft clinging to the side.

"Whoa, this place is empty," Pinché said.

"We might be the only ones here," I replied. "Well, guess we better start drinking."

"Start? Bitch, you need to be cut off."

After dropping off our luggage and putting on suitable pool shorts, it was time for phase two of vacation mode. I crushed up pills of Adderall and made the cutest little lines on the nightstand just above the drawer that held the Bible. I rolled up the last bill from my victory earlier and introduced a line to my brain.

Pinché slid into the pool. I followed diving in. The icy water engulfed my body. The cold silence stabilized my intoxicated mind. I stayed underwater for what felt like an eternity, resurfacing only to take a sip of my drink. The whiskey chased my previously consumed tequila. I could feel the different liquors battling each other in my stomach before they realized they were allies with a common goal. I rested my prone body on the raft, drifting around the pool without a care in the world.

"You drinking more?" I asked Pinché, as he casually finished his cup.

"I got to start getting ready. I can't get all wasted yet like you."

"Amateur."

"Trash."

After spending the rest of the afternoon belligerently intoxicated without anyone kicking us out, we came to the conclusion that we must have been the only people staying at the resort—which was probably best.

I choked either on chlorine water or whiskey, due to possibly passing out while swimming. Unrelated, I decided it was time to get out of the pool. I knocked violently on our hotel room door because Pinché found it funny to lock me out without a towel. My shorts dripped with the cold water.

"Let me in!" I yelled.

"It's unlocked!" Pinché responded.

"It's not working!"

Wearing a complimentary resort robe, looking like Hugh Hefner, Pinché cracked open the window next to the door. "Stop screaming!"

The super strength of the amphetamine kicked my body into high gear. The drugs were the spinach to my Popeye— with only slightly fewer vitamins and minerals. My sun-kissed body lunged at the window. I shoved the glass open nearly shattering it. I hoisted my body onto the windowsill in a single bound. My soaking body stood perched.

"What are you doing?!" Pinché screamed.

I vaulted from the window onto the Bear Queen. We crashed onto the bed behind him. I bounced off his face and ricocheted off the wall, landing on the unforgiving floor. Pinché's robe swung open revealing a wiener flopping around like a fish out of water.

"Where do you tuck that thing?!" I shouted.

"You need a sedative!" Pinché closed his robe. He continued getting ready with showtime looming. I laid lifeless on the king-sized bed when a surprise nap consumed me.

"Get your ass up!"

I was being aggressively woken up by a man wearing nothing but pantyhose and a face full of makeup.

"Get up!"

"Hell no. I'm not going," I mumbled. My body was shaking from the drug-to-food ratio in my body.

"You're going to get your ass up and roll your dying body to the club. We didn't come all this way for you to sleep." Pinché had a way with words. Full of compassion and kindness, I could listen to his soothing voice all day. "Bitch!" He added.

I needed him to stop yelling. The only way to make that happen was to get up. And the only way to get up was with a little motivation. I rolled off the comfortable bed onto the less comfortable floor. I lifted my weak body just enough to reach the top of the nightstand. I shoved Andrew Jackson into a place he was all too familiar with and deployed the sweet chemicals of Adderall into my face.

It felt like an electric shock to my brain. I jumped to my feet. I threw on the nearest piece of clothing and considered myself dressed. I dragged my body to the mirror to make sure I was presentable. I wasn't. But that wasn't going to stop me. My favorite part about day drinking was that when I got ready to go out at night, I always looked good. My judgment was with my inhibitions—drowning somewhere at the bottom of the pool.

We managed to get to Toucan's Tiki Lounge with minutes to spare before showtime. We entered the dressing room that was larger than most bars in L.A. The perimeter of the room was aligned with mirrors and a countertop, not unlike the work room on Rupaul's Drag Race. Vanity lights beamed from above the mirrors, illuminating every crevice of our faces. Despite being in the sun all day, it only took one properly lit room to remind me just how pale I was.

The host of the show was gazing into the mirror next to us. Performers kept filing in. I sat in a rolling chair in the corner, trying not to die.

"At least we made it on time," I told Pinché.

"No thanks to you."

"We're still waiting on one more performer," the host mentioned. "We'll be starting a little late."

"Drag time…" I said, knowing that no drag show in the history of history had ever started on time.

Minutes later, the dressing room door swung open. Ali Doom strutted in wearing a massive white wig. Her voluptuous body swayed like a pin-up model. Her presence exuded high-class sex appeal. Like Pinché, she was proud of her body and took the opportunity to show it off in her performances. Known as the First Lady of Whore Haus, Ali was usually side-by-side with Saint Peter D'vil, hosting events. She was one of very few bio-queens blazing a trail in the underground scene.

All the performers made their way to the main room of Toucan's for showtime.

Ali took the stage while Pinché hung out with me on the sidelines.

"I don't know about biological women doing drag," I confessed to Pinché.

"Are you serious?" He asked.

"Isn't drag supposed to be a place where gay guys are allowed to express themselves?"

"Drag is a place for everyone to express themselves."

"But it's almost unfair," I continued. "Guys work so hard to look beautiful and feminine in drag. Then Ali comes around with a natural feminine beauty without having to do anything."

"Not having to do anything?!" Pinché spouted. "Look at her. Ali is doing extra. She dresses up. She wears a wig on top of her already long hair. She isn't wearing daytime makeup; she's painted like a queen. She lip syncs and wears outrageous outfits just like any other drag queen."

"Yeah… But doesn't she have an advantage looking feminine?"

Pinché pointed at his hairy chest. "Does that look feminine to you?"

I shook my head.

"Drag isn't about looking feminine," he continued. "It's about becoming a character of yourself. It's looks and performance and personality, not who can look the most female."

I watched Ali Doom perform. She moved around the stage with crisp strides. Her towering wig nearly grazed the spotlight above her. Her lip sync exaggerated the song. I realized how wrong I was to think biological females didn't belong in the art. Ali was no different than any other drag queen, regardless of gender. Women were just as much a part of the LGBT+ community as anyone else. Drag was an underground art in the queer community with plenty of room for anyone looking to express themselves.

"Hey, are you okay?" Pinché asked, interrupting my thoughts.

"Huh? Yeah, why?"

"Because you've been staring into nothingness for the longest time."

"Really?" I asked. "Too much Adderall…"

"Yeah…"

I was always aware of my limits and I always made sure to push well beyond them.

We arrived back at the resort after the show. I searched around for the cute front desk guy, but he was nowhere to be found. In fact, nobody was around. The entire resort was as silent and still as the water in the pool.

"So, where did we land on if this place is clothing optional or not?" I asked.

In one impressive swoop, Pinché removed his entire drag

outfit. He stood beneath the starry sky completely naked aside from his fake eyelashes.

"Looks like it's clothing optional," he announced, barreling into the jacuzzi.

"Guess so." I struggled to get my clothes off, nearly falling over in the process.

I submerged into the jacuzzi next to Pinché. We basked beneath the glow of the moon. I was thankful to be tagging along on his drag journey. I was so captivated by his art and he was so appreciative of my support that our partnership of muse and artist was growing. I wasn't sure who was inspiring who. Maybe we were inspiring each other. The only thing that mattered was that we were supporting each other's passions.

A woman with two children raced by us into a room across from ours.

"Hm, guess it's not clothing optional," I shrugged.

THE 'T' IS NOT SILENT

$\mathbf{H}$e was going down on me in a semi-empty theater where Shrek 2 flashed on the screen in front of us. Shrek, Donkey, and a Latin cat—inexplicably wearing boots—disarmed a gang of hoodlums in a magical forest as my genitals were being slobbered on by a guy who, I assumed, hadn't eaten all day. Normally, I would have argued that giant green swamp monsters didn't really set the mood for me, but when you're a fifteen-year-old, oral sex is oral sex.

The gargling noises grew louder and louder. Soon they drowned out the adventure on the screen. The people in the theater were getting annoyed by us. They did that half-turn thing people do in theaters to passively express that we were being too loud. Thankfully, they never turned all the way around.

It was no surprise that Shrek got a star on the Hollywood Walk of Fame. That ogre fought through a lot of adversity in a closed-minded society. It was a relatable story. Sometimes we all felt like that misunderstood creature.

Shrek 2 and I had some things in common: we were both nearing climax and both had ogres in our lives. I looked down to see the guy drowning in his own saliva. His resemblance to Shrek was uncanny. He was a pimple-covered teenager that still retained his baby fat, and hadn't quite learned how to maneuver his posture, so his back hunched over. It was no surprise that his BJ abilities were exquisite, considering he didn't really have much else to offer. He was rude, talked too much, and had a face that should have been banished to a swamp.

The ending of the Academy Award-nominated film was upon us. Pinocchio just revealed that he was wearing a thong, and I started to get anxiety about developing an unwarranted fetish in my subconscious. The last thing I needed was to be turned on by toys wearing lady's undergarments.

My climax commenced. I struggled to muffle a moan that began deep within my recently dropped testicles. The guy drank my fertility and continued fondling my goodies. I tapped his hunchback and had to pry his suction-cup lips off me.

"Shrek is about to win Fiona's parents' approval," I whispered.

Indeed, Shrek was not only gaining acceptance, but he was teaching a valuable lesson about how it was okay to be different. Society should have accepted you for who you were. It was an inspirational theme to a fifteen-year-old boy experiencing his sexuality for the first time. It was also a perfect date-night movie. The ogre did well and so did Shrek.

It was because of that night that my mom learned about my attraction to guys. I accidentally told her the inherently male name of my date when she asked who I was hanging out with. She put two and two together, and I had to admit that I was indeed going out with a guy.

"You know you don't have to hide things from me," my mom said.

I was relieved that she didn't disown me or murder me or, worse, send me to Jesus camp. My mom was pretty accepting of most things, as long as whatever it was I was doing didn't land me in jail. I felt better knowing I could confide in her parts of my life that I hadn't fully understood yet.

"But," she continued, unexpectedly, "I know in my heart that you are not actually attracted to guys."

That was devastating to hear. I thought mothers were supposed to know everything. I thought they were supposed to have all the answers in the world. But, for the first time in my life, she was wrong, and I knew it.

*   *   *

A couple years had passed since that marvelous date and, subsequently, me coming out to my mom. She became more and more accepting of my sexuality when she realized that it was permanent and she didn't have much of a choice.

On one of the three days that it rained in Southern California that year, Milo and his girlfriend Lauren were hanging out with me in my room. The three of us were trading off playing Mario Kart. Well, they kept trading off because I was unbeatable. Just as I was going to obliterate Milo's hope-filled grasp on first place with a spiked shell, I heard my mom pulling into the driveway. I vacated my throne of dominance to greet her.

"Hope it's okay that I have a couple friends over," I said to my mom as I helped her carry groceries into the house.

"Sure," she said. "I need to meet them, though. What's on your face?" She wiped the highlight off my cheek that I had spent a half hour on trying to make look subtle.

She started toward my room.

"Wait!" I shouted. "There's something I should tell you first."

She stared into my eyes, trying to read if they were on drugs.

"Both of my friends that are here are transgender."

"Okay..." She replied, not completely sure what that meant.

It was one thing to tell my mom about my own sexuality. It was another thing for her to meet a trans person for the first time. Introducing my trans friends to anyone had the potential to be a shocking moment if the person wasn't familiar with the

LGBT+ world.

My mom entered my room to find a guy and a girl playing video games. Milo and Lauren both greeted her with a hug and introduced themselves before returning to Mario Kart. My mom closed the door and turned back to me.

"I thought you said they were transgender?" She asked.

"They are," I replied.

"I don't know why you felt the need to warn me. You made it seem like they were going to be weird or something. They look like regular kids to me."

I was relieved that she didn't mind me having queer people over. Then I was happy that she couldn't tell or didn't care about the difference between how my friends looked compared to their assigned genders at birth. It was reassuring to hear someone be so accepting especially when it was my own family.

"Hey," my mom continued, "can I borrow your foundation? I ran out yesterday."

I smiled. "Top drawer in the restroom."

*   *   *

Milo, Lauren, and I hung out quite a bit. It was spring semester in college and we all went to the same school. Like any other freshmen, we spent our days avoiding classes and getting stoned on the bleachers of the baseball field.

Eventually, Milo was one-missed class away from having his financial aid revoked. That afternoon, he decided to go to class while Lauren and I spent the next few hours together.

We strolled around the field enjoying each other's company, talking about nothing in particular. We found a nice patch of grass to sit on when I noticed the way the sun reflected off her captivating brown eyes. They were like kaleidoscopes of different shades, peeking from beneath her long hair. Her skin was milky and smooth from the hormones she was taking. I looked up at her entrancing smile that boasted two snakebite piercings.

"I can't believe you didn't know I was trans when you met

me," Lauren said.

"Milo used female pronouns with you. I just followed suit without even thinking about it," I replied. "I could only assume you were female."

She blushed, happy that I saw her for who she was.

"Do you think I'm pretty?" She asked.

"I think you're stunning," I replied.

"Even though I wasn't born female?"

"Makes no difference to me."

She blushed. Her eyelashes fluttered. An angelic smile drifted across her face. I leaned in pressing my lips against hers without even realizing what I was doing. Our warm lips connected with euphoria. I could taste the metal from her piercings. I pulled away just as quickly.

"What—" She started.

"I'm sorry," I cut her off. "I don't know what happened."

She leaned back into me, returning her lips to mine. The endorphins in my brain bursted out of their cage, flooding my body. I felt weightless. She was the most beautiful woman I had ever kissed. But that happiness was quickly overshadowed by regret.

"We can't," she stopped me.

I sighed knowing exactly why.

Milo and Lauren broke up shortly after that day. I wasn't sure if it was entirely my fault, but there was no way that me kissing my friend's girlfriend helped their already rocky relationship in any way. Despite the breakup and the strange love triangle that I wasn't completely sure Milo was even aware of, he and I remained friends. However, Lauren got kicked out of Milo's house. With nowhere to go, I took Lauren in to live with me.

I was enjoying her sleeping in my bed and waking up to her face in the mornings. Her cold, smooth skin felt incredible when it brushed against mine. Although I didn't have as much room in my bed as when I slept alone, it was much more enjoyable to have someone next to me.

A week later, I drove Lauren back to Milo's house to pick

up the remainder of her belongings.

"Let's get this over with," I said.

"I'll get my stuff fast. There's not much," Lauren replied.

As she went inside the house, Milo came out to greet me.

"Hey," he said.

"Hi," I responded awkwardly.

We stood in silence waiting for Lauren to finish gathering her belongings.

"Well," I said to Milo, "let's hang soon."

Lauren spent another couple of weeks with me. We bonded over absolutely nothing because we didn't have a single thing in common. I was blinded by her seductive charisma and I gave her the comfort of my parents' roof over her head. But that wasn't enough to allow us to continue to play House. Lauren refused to look for a job or go to school or do anything with her life. Despite my protests of being in love and wanting to be happy, my parents decided to kick her out of the house.

Lauren and I did some research to try to find a shelter for her to stay at since she refused to return to live with her family for reasons I didn't ask. That's when I found the Los Angeles LGBT Youth Center that provided housing for homeless youth. That seemed like the best—and only—option for her. I didn't want her to leave, but we didn't have a choice.

I drove Lauren up the 101 freeway. Her personal belongings dwindled down to whatever she could cram into a single trash bag. She stared pensively out the window. She was undoubtedly feeling the rejection of Milo, my family, and the rest of the world. She was a lost kid that I desperately wanted to save, but I didn't have the power to help someone when I didn't even know what my own place in the world was yet.

"Don't you want to be with me?" She asked, finally breaking the unbearable silence.

"Of course I do," I answered. "But it just can't happen right now. You're going to be so far away, and we both have to figure out how to get our lives together."

"But I need you."

Her words cut deep through me. All I ever wanted to do was help people, especially those in my community. But I didn't know what else I could do. I pulled up to the LGBT Center. I slowly walked Lauren in, trying to savor every moment that would soon disappear. Our lives were being split in different directions. It broke my heart to part ways, not only with someone that I developed feelings for, but with someone that felt just as alone in the world as I did.

The lady at the front desk welcomed us with a kind smile, but nothing could dissolve the heavy cloud above us. We were two queer kids unsure of where we belonged in the world.

Lauren looked at me with tears in her eyes.

"I'm sorry," I said.

"I'll miss you," she replied.

Milo and I remained friends. In fact, we grew even closer together than I had ever expected. Without the allure of Lauren in our lives, there was nothing to break our bond. We became as close as brothers and would never let another person get in the way of that. We were there for each other. Milo was there helping me clean after every party at my parents' house; he was there the first time I hallucinated; and I was there for him when his body dysphoria struck.

The summer after Milo had his top surgery was the most celebrated. It was the first time he felt comfortable enough to take off his shirt while swimming. We lounged around his pool all day, soaking in the sun.

"You know I'm really sorry about the whole Lauren situation, right?" I asked.

"What?" He responded.

"I did really like her. And I didn't think you and I would become this close."

"Oh. It's cool. I'm not worried about it."

"No, but I'm really sorry. I love you so much and you're one of my best friends."

"I love you too," he replied.

"I'm sorry I had sex with her. She was hot, but that's no excuse," I continued.

"Wait, you had sex with her?"

"I just feel like you're not over it and I'm really sorry."

"Well, stop bringing it up!"

"Okay, okay, you're right," I admitted. "But, I just feel like you're not over it. What if I let you punch me? How about one free—"

BAM!

Without hesitation, Milo punched me straight in the face before I could even finish my sentence. Thankfully, standing in the pool helped maintain my balance, otherwise I would have been on the floor. I could feel my cheek swell immediately. The next day, the entire side of my face was swollen. The inside of my cheek had a cut that was trying to scab but kept reopening every time I ate. The taste of iron plagued my mouth for my next few meals.

The punch solidified two things. First, that getting hit in the face was not nearly as poetic as it was in the movies. Second, that my friendship with Milo grew even stronger that day. If one of your best friends doesn't punch you in the face at least once, then you're not truly best friends.

*   *   *

I drove back to the LGBT Center to visit Lauren. I nervously approached the steps leading up to the Center. I was terrified that she turned to drugs or hated me or any number of other justified scenarios. Before I could reach the door, an extraordinarily stunning woman sauntered out. Lauren wore a long, orange sundress that flowed from her tall body. Her hair was cut short with Auburn streaks, her snakebite piercings were a fresh black, and her smile beamed an unparalleled beauty.

"Why are you looking at me like that?" She asked.

"I don't think I've ever seen you wear a dress before," I replied. I couldn't stop staring at her. An uncontrollable grin stained my face.

"I've never owned a dress before," she replied. "They have donated clothes here in the Center. It was the only one that fit my size."

"It looks incredible. You look so happy."

"I am," she said smiling. "Thank you."

I had never seen Lauren so happy before. I had never seen anyone in my life radiate such happiness as she did wearing that dress. The LGBT Center was there for her when nobody else was; they took care of her when I couldn't. Not only did they give her a place to live, but they showed her that she could be happy with who she was.

Whoever took the time to donate that dress had no idea that they had changed someone's life. The person that donated that article of clothing would never know that they helped a kid become comfortable in their own body for the first time.

Every year after that day, I went around to my friends and family asking for any clothes to donate to the LGBT Center. I would make my annual rounds picking up clothing of all shapes and sizes. My car would be full of bags packed with clothes. Then, I would drive to the Center where kids would assist me in lugging the bags in. The front desk person would always ask if I wanted to leave my name to which I would decline.

I was paying forward the good deed that someone contributed before me. All I could hope for was that maybe another lost person would be able to find something in those bags that made them smile the way Lauren did.

I could never express enough gratitude to whoever the person was that donated the orange dress. Thank you for helping Lauren find her smile.

METH

"**B**itch, I can't fit!" Isadora shouted from the half of his body that was inside the car.

"Suck it in!" I yelled, trying to shove him in.

He was like a big, homosexual Winnie the Pooh—one end in the car, the other stuck outside. That would have been a more accurate character for him to portray in that night's Disney-themed Wepa challenge. Instead, he settled on Ursula. Tentacles hung out the door beating me in the face; purple body paint rubbed onto me. My sweat started to drip.

"Hurry up! We're going to be late," the buried head of Isadora said.

With all my strength, I shoved the big, purple queen into the backseat of the car. His tentacles slid with him; his body thumped against the opposite door.

"Jesus! I'm a lady!" Isadora growled.

I wasn't sure if he was right-side up or upside down, but Isadora Manson was in the car.

"You ready for this?" I asked.

"For what?"

With the tiniest gap between Isadora's body and the open

door, I leaped in. I shoved myself into drag queen crevices that I wished to never visit again. My face was mashed into Isadora's cleavage. His tentacles grazed my no-no zone. The car was filled with an oversized outfit, oversized hair, and an oversized ass.

Isadora's drag sisters sat comfortably in the front seats, driving us to the venue.

"At least you won't lose by being late," I said.

"I'm not going to lose at all," Isadora corrected.

"Well, don't be disappointed if you do. I'm still proud of you for making it this far."

Isadora cocked his head away from being buried in the door. "You think I'm going to get eliminated?"

"No. It's not that. It's just, this is a really bulky costume. I don't even know how you're going to walk. Plus all these other queens bring such high-energy performances."

"Girl, I can't believe you're doubting me."

"You're still a new queen," I continued. "I don't want you to get your feelings hurt. I think this is a really good learning experience for you. For later competitions."

"Whatever."

We rushed into Faultline in time for the competition. I hadn't meant to disclose my doubts to Isadora. I assumed that he already knew he was a long shot for winning the competition. Contrary, he was only focused on the victory and shut out any other possibilities.

I secured a spot in front of the stage while people filed into the venue for the Disney-themed night.

"Hey!" Tristan screeched from a table. "You ready for Isadora to beat some bitches?"

"It's not going to be that easy," I replied.

"Of course it is. It's Isadora. She's the best. I wouldn't be friends with a loser."

The competition commenced. The field of performers was narrowing, leaving only high-quality performances. That night had everything from Alice's white rabbit lip syncing to Jefferson Airplane's song of the same name, to a prosthetic-billed Daisy Duck, to a surprisingly pedestrian Pocahontas from Dayshawna.

Then came Isadora.

The Ursula queen waddled his way to the center of the stage with his tentacles tied up around him. He focused on each step, careful to not tumble over. Then the music hit. He lip synced to Ursula's song sprinkled with the character's evil dialogue. Then, Isadora swayed toward the stairs trying to maintain his balance. My chest clenched with anxiety.

He gingerly made his way down the steps toward the audience. He lugged around the outfit, trying to perform to the crowd. He was spending a lot of time and energy on navigating the costume. Finally, he climbed back onto the stage. It was a lackluster performance for such an elaborate wardrobe, and I was still praying he wouldn't fall.

The Disney villain's song drifted away. Isadora's drag sisters unhooked his tentacles, allowing them to flow to their three-foot-long potential. His sisters pointed toy guns around him that unleashed a cavalcade of bubbles.

CLICK. CLICK. CLICK.

The song transitioned to the next. The crowd and judges erupted with cheers, recognizing the song immediately. It was a song by legendary drag queen Divine—the artist whom the original Ursula character was based on. Divine was a cult icon that pioneered the alternative drag scene. Without him forcing his way through barriers and pummeling glass ceilings, there would have been no underground drag scene.

The audience rose to their feet. The judges followed. Isadora's expression twisted, contorted, and transformed. He became the Divine character right before our eyes. The snarl, the disgust, and the evil came to life. He radiated emotion. He exuded confidence. Most importantly, Isadora's smile showed everyone that he was having fun.

I lowered my phone from recording. I gazed around witnessing the crowd being engulfed in the pageantry. All my anxieties for Isadora disappeared. For the first time in the competition, my Dance Mom nerves settled. I was finally able to relax and genuinely enjoy the show.

I watched Isadora bounce around in the bubbles. I laughed at the outrageousness of his wig, the purple glitter covering his skin, and the eight ridiculously long tentacles dangling from his body. It was outlandish. That form of art was so over the top and entertaining.

I finally understood why we loved watching men in dresses pretend to sing songs. It was pure fun. It made me forget all the problems in the world as I got lost in the insanity. Up until that moment, I was just a friend coming to support Isadora. But that performance turned me into a fan. I didn't feel a personal connection during those three minutes. Instead, I just enjoyed being entertained.

Isadora concluded his number to a well-deserved round of applause.

After the rest of the competitors performed, Robbie Osa brought them back to the stage to announce the winner of the night.

"There's no way he's going to be eliminated," I whispered to Tristan. "I hope."

Isadora stood with confidence. Robbie Osa announced that Isadora was safe from elimination and a runner-up to the winner. Although the audience felt like Isadora should have been the winner of that challenge, no decision could kill the euphoria we got from watching his performance. It was the best performance Isadora had ever put together.

In a surprising twist, Dayshawna Rose and Britney Shears —the two highest-quality performers—were put in the bottom. They went head-to-head in an intense lip sync battle. They brought worthy performances in an attempt to stay in the competition. Robbie Osa returned to the stage once they concluded.

"Dayshawna," Robbie began, "you've been turning out these performances week after week, but I'm not sure what happened tonight. I'm sorry, Dayshawna, but you are eliminated."

A stunned silence drifted over the audience. The competitors were stunned. I was stunned. The biggest threat in the competition was eliminated.

"Holy balls," I said to Tristan. "Isadora has a chance. He actually has a chance."

"Told you."

It felt surreal to say it out loud. Not only was the top contender eliminated, but there were only four competitors left. Isadora may not have been a clear favorite, but at least now everyone was on the same par.

As he descended the stage, people in the audience ran up to congratulate him. The gleam of Isadora's smile beamed throughout the room. He was proud of himself and enjoying every second of the adulation. His smile was well deserved.

Isadora had a chance.

*   *   *

"I would never eat someone's ass!" Isadora gasped, placing a hand to his chest.

The roar of the ocean waves carried his voice toward a group of suburban moms. Malibu wasn't exactly where we belonged (we were more of a trashy Venice Beach crowd), but there was free parking and sand devoid of broken glass.

"I'm a classy lady," Isadora continued.

"Our generation invented eating ass or at least we're not afraid to admit it," I replied.

A suburban mom working on a leathery tan glanced over at us. She was probably in her forties, but her skin looked sixty while her breasts were in their infant years.

"Tristan always tells me how he does that. That's disgusting."

I rolled my eyes. "So you're really welcoming him into your life again?"

"I have to. He doesn't have anyone else. You haven't seen that he has changed?"

I couldn't lie. "I guess. He was pretty put together the last few times he came to watch you perform."

"See. He's fine. He's been through a lot, girl."

"I know," I agreed. "But so have you. I've never seen you so happy as you have been lately with drag. I just don't want you to throw it all away trying to help someone that doesn't want help."

"Like I said, things are different now. He's been hanging out with my family lately. Did I tell you my mom found out I'm a drag queen?"

"What?! Are you serious?" I gasped.

"We haven't talked about it yet. I walked in on her watching one of my performances on the computer."

"Your mom secretly watches your performances?"

"I guess so."

I reached over to give Isadora a hug. The Leather Face suburban mom stared at us.

*   *   *

We were a couple days away from the next Wepa challenge. Isadora and I spent some time apart to enjoy the stress-free days. The next challenge was going to be the most important one thus far. It would determine which queens would compete in the finale.

My phone rang as I threw a load of laundry into the washer. As a millennial, I had a pretty strict "don't answer the phone" rule. There was nothing that needed to be said in a phone call that couldn't be said in a text. However, it was unusual for Tristan to be calling me. I picked up.

"They're following me! They're fucking following me!" Tristan screamed through the phone.

"What? Who's following you? Where are you?" I asked.

"They want to kill me! Get them away!"

"Where are you?" I panicked.

"Driving. In L.A."

CLICK.

The phone hung up before I could say anything more. My hands shook when I tried calling him back. No answer. I tried again. No answer. The worst scenarios flashed through my mind. I called once more.

Tristan picked up.

"What the hell is going on?!" I demanded.

"They're following me," he repeated.

"Who? Where are you? Come to my place. You can hang here and we can—"

CLICK.

He hung up again. I stepped out of my millennial comfort zone, dialing another number.

"Hey, someone is trying to murder your best friend or something. I think he's drunk," I said into the phone.

"He called me too," Isadora remarked. "He's probably on meth again."

"Oh, just meth," I said, relieved.

"What do you mean just meth?"

"It means there's probably not really anyone chasing him. Just paranoia."

"And you think that's better?!"

"I guess he shouldn't be driving like that."

"No shit!" Isadora cried out of breath.

"What are you doing?"

"I was practicing for Wepa, but I got to go find Tristan."

"You can't," I countered. "You've got your own stuff to focus on."

"Are you serious? Right now is not the time for you to be an asshole. I'm not going to put this competition over my friend."

"Maybe I am being an asshole. Maybe Tristan is being an asshole for expecting you to put his awful choices before your own life."

"He needs help," Isadora said flatly.

"Then I'll go find him."

"But—"

"He's calling me right now," I lied.

I hung up with Isadora then frantically tried calling Tristan again. I stared at my black clothes spinning in the washer as the phone rang. I had no plans other than doing laundry that night, but I really didn't want to invest time in searching for someone tweaking in Hollywood. It would be like trying to find a needle in a needle stack.

Voicemail picked up.

I got ready to go searching for him. The only clothes I had clean were the forgotten ones in the back of my closet that I hadn't seen since High School. I threw on the first thing I grabbed—a PopTart shirt with a singing dinosaur on it and oversized track pants with a button missing from the crotch. I tried not to complain, though. I was pretty sure other people were having a worse day.

"Help! They're following me!" Tristan shouted again when he finally picked up the phone.

"Why don't you come to my place. You're in L.A. right?" I asked.

Tristan started bawling.

"Are you at least pulled over? I really don't think you should be driving right now."

"I'm going home," he sniffled. "I want to say 'bye' to my mom before I die."

Holy Christ. If I hadn't already decided not to touch methamphetamine, that sentence would have definitely convinced me.

"That's probably best," I told him. "Can you text me when you get home?"

"Yeah."

"All right. I'm going to finish doing my laundry. You should probably stop doing meth and try not to die."

It was pretty sound advice for anyone, really.

*   *   *

Isadora was accelerating to near triple digits on Santa Monica Boulevard—a feat that would have been impressive if I wasn't fearing for my life. He barely dodged parked cars, potholes, and pedestrians. Strangely, the drag queen thought I was being dramatic every time I tried to tell him he was a terrible driver. I gripped the front seat, bracing myself for potential impact.

"You're going to kill us," I moaned.

"We can't be late."

"We do this every night. We've never actually been late to

Wepa."

The Queen of Emotion continued speeding. We pulled into the Faultline parking lot officially late, and he didn't even have nails on yet. Isadora found gloves to throw on and cinched his wig as best he could before running his heels into the venue.

I rushed in behind him when I ran into Spoons.

"You guys are late," he said.

"Yes. Thank you, dear, for reminding me."

"What's going on?"

I sighed. "I think he's lost focus."

"But he's so close."

The audience's cheers roared when Isadora climbed the stage but faded throughout the performance. He had been struggling all week to come up with an idea for his number before finally settling on something the night before. He couldn't figure out what to wear, so he threw various fabrics together hoping for the best. He couldn't decide on music quick enough to have a professional mix it together, so he mixed it himself. The audio was grainy and skipped. His outfit was ripped at the seams. The performance concluded with a dull clap from the audience.

After the competitors finished, Robbie Osa strutted onto the DJ platform.

"Ladies and gentlemen, we here at Wepa believe in second chances. We believe it's possible for a performer to have a bad night, and they shouldn't be judged based on that when all of their other performances were incredible."

I smiled hoping Isadora caught a break.

"So please welcome back… Dayshawna Rose!"

The audience erupted for the returning queen. Everyone in the building was ecstatic to see the high-energy Dayshawna back in the competition. Everyone except Spoons and me.

"Not good," I whispered.

"Nope," Spoons agreed.

"And as a bonus for coming back," Robbie continued, "we're giving Dayshawna the opportunity to eliminate one of the competitors to decide who the final three will be in the finale.

"Shit," I lamented a little too loud.

Robbie passed the microphone to Dayshawna. "It was Britney Shears who eliminated me when I was in the bottom two. If I wanted to be a bitch, I could return the favor. But, on the other hand, Isadora is my biggest threat in the competition..."

I was surprised. Isadora and Dayshawna had completely different styles of drag, but the High-Desert Queen recognized they were both fierce, entertaining competitors. He saw that Isadora had fought his way to get himself to the same level.

"But," Dayshawna continued, "I think I'll keep those two. I'd like to face them in the finale." He decided to eliminate the fourth competitor onstage.

"Oh my god," I said to Spoons. "Do you know what this means? Isadora just made it to the finale. Isadora is competing in the finale!"

All I had hoped for, was that Isadora wouldn't be eliminated first. Then, he forced me to recognize that he was a viable threat in the competition. Now, the surreal thought was suddenly reality: Isadora couldn't get any closer to the end without winning. Everything he had worked so hard for was paying off. He was in the finale of the Wepa competition.

When the competitors descended the stage, they were bombarded by people congratulating them. Isadora extended cold hugs to the people that approached him. He made his way toward Spoons and me.

"I didn't do good tonight," Isadora shrugged with exhaustion.

"Isadora, you've made it to the finale. This is what it has all been about."

"I know," he replied flatly. "I've got to go take off all this drag. I have work in a few hours."

For the first time in the competition, Isadora left the venue without me.

CABBAGE PATCH QUEEN

He stood beneath the frame of my doorway. A wig rested on top of his head. Eyelashes extended from his beady eyes. His lips were deliciously overdrawn. Below the fully transformed head, hung broad shoulders. His lower body boasted the chic swap-meet couture of basketball shorts and chanclas.

This was the void between a man and a drag queen. It was the abyss that few people got to witness. He was becoming a girl but was still not yet a woman.

I had to remind myself that Isadora was my friend. Which meant I had to love him before, after, and even during his transformation into a drag queen every night.

"Stop taking pictures," Isadora commanded.

"I can't help it. This is terrifying."

My apartment was covered with the usual drag queen paraphernalia plus a few extra articles. 99-Cent Store items were scheduled to be included in Isadora's performance. He was pulling out all the stops for the Wepa Finale. Tinsel covered the couches; feathers were strewn all around. I moved some fabric in an attempt to sit on the couch. However, beneath the fabric rested a pile of vegetables.

"Why is there lettuce?" I asked.

"Don't be stupid," Isadora answered. "It's cabbage."

"Oh."

At that point, I learned not to question Isadora any further. He powered his way through the competition, getting himself to the finale. If he had a plan to use the giant green vegetable, then he had my full support.

My phone illuminated, releasing a small amount of endorphins in my brain because—like a true millennial—text messages triggered my happiness. I checked my phone only to be disappointed that it was not the message I was waiting for. I really didn't care that GrubHub wanted me to rate the food they just delivered. They should have known they deserved five stars. My stomach was full, and I didn't have to move more than five feet from my couch. I would have given them six stars if I could.

I was anxiously waiting for my coworker to text me back. I needed my shift covered at work that night. I didn't think Isadora would make it to the finale, so I never bothered to request the night off.

Normally, I would have just called in sick. But, because of my frequent hangovers that I usually called out for, I was already on thin ice at work. In no uncertain terms, my manager let me know that I would not be welcomed back if I missed another day of work.

My work may not have always played by legal rules—like most companies that expect maximum effort from poorly paid employees—but it was that job that allowed me to use my car for driving rather than for living in. It was the paychecks from that job that let me put a real roof over my head. Plus, I was able to afford all the bland Subway sandwiches I wanted without the fear of my credit card declining.

I stared at my phone, hoping my coworker would text me back to take my shift.

"Is that Spoons?" Isadora asked.

"No, why?"

"I haven't heard from him."

"Is he supposed to come tonight?"

"He better! He's in my performance. If he doesn't show up, you're going to have to be in it," he warned.

I ignored the request.

"Where's that from?" I asked about a long, flowing gown he was trying on.

"It's from my mom."

"Your mom bought you a dress?" I asked, surprised.

"No, she made it for me. Sewed it by hand."

"You went from being terrified of your parents finding out about you doing drag, to your mom helping you with outfits?"

"Yeah."

"You don't realize just how amazing that is, do you?"

"Don't make me cry, girl. My makeup."

Isadora finished putting on the final touches of his drag. He stepped away from the mirror. His heels glided toward me, using the living room as a runway. His steps were crisp and flowed comfortably. His dress accentuated his body with the middle cinched to create a curvy illusion. His chest was squeezed together creating his trademark breasts that had developed from D-cups to solid G's.

He continued strutting underneath the light, illuminating his makeup. His contour was sleek, giving shape to his apple cheeks. His eyebrows were perfectly hidden beneath the ones he drew on. They exuded melodramatic, telenovela realness. At the end of the runway, he drifted his hand below his chin allowing his jewelry to sparkle.

"Ready," the Queen of Emotion elegantly announced.

"We've still got like an hour before we have to be there," I said.

"I'm not trying to be late to the finale."

"After an entire summer of rushing to make it on time, you've finally decided to get there early," I huffed.

"Stop being so dramatic. You ready or what?"

I rolled my eyes then threw on a hat and pants. It took me much less time to get ready than Isadora. We headed toward the door.

"Oh, I almost forgot!" Isadora ran back grabbing the cabbage.

We didn't race to the car. We didn't rush to chug drinks. I didn't shove Isadora into the backseat. And, thankfully, Isadora didn't speed all the way to the venue. He was focused on winning the competition and was leaving nothing to chance.

We casually entered the venue. A crowd of people was already forming. The bartenders hurried to make drinks. Isadora rolled in his suitcase full of costumes, props, and vegetables. He headed toward the backstage area to meet up with his backup dancers and other performers in his number. Spoons was still nowhere to be seen.

My phone vibrated. It was a text message from my coworker:

Sorry, I won't be able to cover for you.

I was desperate. I couldn't lose my job, but I also couldn't abandon Isadora. I replied:

Please. I'm really sick.

They answered:

Yeah, right. You just want to go to that dumb drag show. I saw your post on IG.

Fuck social media and my inability to not post snippets of my life.

Rapid flashbacks of living in my car raced through my mind. The thought of not being able to pay for food made me shutter. I thought how maybe it wouldn't be as difficult to find a job as it was before. I reminded myself that was exactly what I thought the last time. I didn't have a choice. I was going to have to leave the competition early to go to work.

I had been there for all the other nights of the competition. I lent Isadora my entire apartment to use as his own personal dressing room before every performance. I even went to his side gigs, and we enjoyed each other's company on our days off. I felt like I paid my debt to Isadora for helping me when I was at my lowest point. I no longer owed him anything. Besides, he was so focused on the competition that he wouldn't even notice if I snuck out.

As I was staring at the glow from my phone, a short figure came up to me with a beaming smile.

"Milo!" I shouted, wrapping my arms around him. "What are you doing here?!"

"I wasn't going to miss Isadora winning the competition," Milo replied. "Besides, I had to bring that guy." He pointed across the room. Spoons was staggering around before he noticed us staring. A squeal of excitement escaped him as he hoisted me above his head like Simba.

"You're wasted, aren't you?" I asked, inhaling the scent of tequila on his breath.

"Yup!" He admitted.

"Isadora is going crazy thinking you bailed. You better go backstage and find him."

"When was the last time we were all together like this?" Milo asked.

"Years," Spoons replied.

"We all kind of went our separate ways," I said.

"Who would have thought that we would all come back together because of Isadora's drag?" Milo asked.

Spoons pulled us together with his massive arms, nearly squeezing the life out of me.

"You big asshole," I scolded. "Go find Isadora!"

He released his death grip before disappearing behind the stage. Milo found the bar while I remained with my phone in my hand. I took a deep breath before texting my coworker back:

I'm not going in for my shift tonight.

There was no way I wasn't going to be there to see Isadora's performance. Even my best friends showed up to support him. I wasn't going to give up my opportunity to witness Isadora live his dream. I wasn't going to miss out on seeing the insecure kid I met years ago transform into a confident performer. I didn't owe him anything. Staying there was going to be for me.

My coworker responded with the middle finger Emoji followed by the smiling poop. I exhaled, accepting that I would once again be out of a job. At least this time, it was going to be for a good reason. I put away my phone and replaced it with a drink. I might as well have tried to enjoy the rest of the night.

The door to the venue swung open, allowing a gust of the late-summer air to rush in. I peered over my drink to see Tristan strolling in with his head held high. He waved around at people that stared back not knowing who he was. I tried to avoid eye contact, but it was too late.

"I knew you'd be here!" Tristan exclaimed.

"Yeah," I replied.

"Man, the other night was crazy."

"Mm."

"But it's okay now. I'm not doing meth ever again. Only poppers. Want to have sex later?"

"Tristan, you shouldn't be here. Isadora is doing amazing in—"

"Of course I should be here! Isadora needs me. She'd be lost without me."

Before I could respond, the DJ lowered the music. Robbie Osa graced the stage, ready to introduce the first competitor.

Isadora made his entrance to a song by Missy Elliott. Following behind him was half a dozen backup dancers including Spoons. Isadora was going to have to leap way out of his comfort zone in order to pull off that number.

The hip-hop song built up. Isadora and his dancers moved in sync. They had been practicing nonstop since the last challenge and it showed. Isadora hustled around the stage unlike any big queen I had ever seen before. For someone that smoked half a pack of cigarettes that day, he maintained his stamina. If he was winded even for a second, he didn't express it.

My phone vibrated in the middle of the performance. A message from my coworker popped up:

I took your shift. You owe me. Have fun seeing guys in dresses.

I smiled. It didn't matter if nobody understood the art of drag that I grew to love, but they at least knew it was important to me.

I put my arm around Milo. We watched as Spoons held together his intoxication just long enough to fulfill his part. The performance ended and Isadora rejoined us with a razor-sharp focus. The wheels in his head were turning. He was simultaneously dissecting the performance he just finished while also thinking about the choreography for his next number.

"Do you need a drink?" I asked. "Or a water or—"

"Look bitch, I'm here!" Tristan interrupted.

"Not now, Tristan," Isadora replied. He turned back to me. "I have to go get ready for the next number."

"Cool, I'll come with you," Tristan interjected. "Let me fix those eyebrows. I can do them way better than you."

I turned to Tristan. Before I could say a word, Isadora stepped in.

"Look, Tristan," Isadora began, "you can come to my shows to support me all you want. I can't stop you from going somewhere. But when I'm in drag, it's not about you. Especially not tonight. I've worked too hard and come too far to have you keep bringing me down."

"I was in the hospital the other day," Tristan continued. "You didn't even come see me."

"From the meth you chose to do?!" Isadora shouted. "I can't keep being held back by trying to help you when you don't even want to help yourself. I have to get ready now."

Isadora turned around, marching to the back of the stage with a toxic weight lifted from his shoulders. Tristan looked at me with swelling eyes but forced a tough-guy facade.

"Fuck that bitch." He chugged the rest of his drink and stormed out of the venue.

Milo and I took our spots on the side of the stage next to Isadora's drag sisters. The other two finalists—Britney Shears and Dayshawna Rose—performed their songs with the execution and precision one would expect in the finale. Dayshawna brought the high energy he was notorious for and Britney Shears brought a flawless routine with professional backup dancers.

Isadora performed his second number. The challenge for that one was to incorporate the random 99-Cent Store items that Robbie Osa provided the queens. That explained all the tinsel and feathers in my apartment. Isadora performed Katy Perry's "Bon Appétit". I was relieved to finally understand why he had so many vegetables with him.

He played the role of a turkey being put into an oven. Spoons shaved carrots and other phallic food items onto the Queen of Emotion. The number concluded with Spoons squirting the big queen with a turkey baster.

"If I was the host of the competition," one of the judges began. "I would have disqualified you for making such a mess on the stage."

The stage was annihilated with food and liquid. Thankfully, a shirtless Spoons helped clean up the mess and simultaneously distracted the swooning judges.

Once the stage was clean, Robbie Osa returned wary of any remnants of gravy. "Ladies and gentlemen, I'd like to bring out all of our finalists: Britney Shears, Dayshawna Rose, and Isadora Manson."

Spoons put a vegetable-covered arm around me. I squeezed Milo's hand. Isadora and I had come a long way from going to a dingy little club in the Inland Empire to see Raven perform. Now Isadora was the performer I was going out to see. That was the moment he had been working so hard for all summer. The numerous hours spent on hair and makeup, the amount of sleep lost from going to work after shows, the countless late-night texts from Isadora about performance ideas had all led to that moment.

"The winner of the Wepa competition is… Dayshawna Rose!"

Isadora's face dropped. I could hear the air rush out of his body. I could feel his heart being crushed. We knew from the beginning that Dayshawna was the biggest threat—her dance moves, charisma, and ability to captivate a crowd was untouchable. There was no shame in losing to a queen of that caliber. He earned his victory and nobody could say different.

Isadora graciously hugged the other competitors. He descended the stage into the arms of strangers and friends congratulating him on making it to the finale. He disappeared backstage to collect his belongings.

Spoons, Milo, Isadora's drag sisters, the backup dancers, and I trudged somberly with the Queen of Emotion toward his car. We helped him put all his props and luggage into the trunk.

"I love you, and I'm so proud. This was the best summer of my life," I told him.

"I'm going to miss coming over to do my makeup," Isadora admitted.

"You never have to do makeup in your car again."

We all stood around the parking lot. The Wepa competition was over. There was nothing left to say. Isadora struggled to get his final bag into his car. He opened it, pulling out a giant green head of cabbage.

"Oh my god, I forgot to even use this!" Isadora hoisted the innocent piece of produce into the air and obliterated it on the concrete. "Fuck this lettuce!"

PART IV

MEAN THREESOME

It was a dark, stormy Southern California night. Which meant the sky cast down just enough moisture to put my windshield wipers on the lowest setting for the better part of twenty minutes. Despite the quantity, it was still dangerous to be driving because Los Angeles drivers were clueless on how to function in such treacherous conditions. Dismissing the thought of a collision—or worse, rain traffic—I stayed focused on my mission.

I was on my way to a booty call. I had a pretty strict "toot it and boot it" rule where I only had sex with a person one time and never contacted them again. This guy, however, was different. No, this wasn't a story of my teenage self suddenly falling for a one-night stand. This was not some kind of slutty Lifetime movie. Instead, I found myself driving to his house again because he wanted to add a third person to our dynamic.

I had never had a threesome with all guys before. I was feeling particularly adventurous so I thought, why not? I had seen plenty of threesomes in porn. How different could the real thing have been?

The guy that set up that night's romp swamp had the best occupation of anyone I had ever slept with. He beat out the janitor, the crystal-ball psychic, and the guy that managed a PetCo. This particular guy was a pilot, and I was happy to admit that I had never forgot his name because I had never even known what it was.

I had no idea who the new person was that would be joining us. I had no description, no picture, no résumé. I didn't know what position he played or if there was anything off-limits. As if I wasn't nervous enough entering my first threesome, I didn't even know who was going to be touching my naughty bits.

I pulled up to the impressive house resting at the end of a family-friendly cul-de-sac. I was already running late, but I needed another minute to collect myself. My hands were sweating despite the freezing temperature of fifty-four degrees.

I reached to turn up the heater when my hand knocked into a small glass pipe that was sitting in the CD storage slot. I nodded to myself in the mirror.

There was only remnants of weed in the bowl, but I was determined to scrape enough of the ashes to be able to light it up. I searched around the trash-infested car for something sharp. I rummaged through hamburger wrappers to find a broken piece of plastic from a pen.

I scraped the bowl with determination, pulling up enough marijuana crumbs to catch fire. I lit the bowl, inhaling as deeply as I could. The wonderful, dry taste filled my mouth. I inhaled again, feeling the clumps of dirt and ash smoke enter my lungs. I hit it once more and waited for the coughing to subside.

I had pre-gamed a lot of events in my life, but I never thought I'd pre-game a threesome. I hoped I smoked enough to feel relaxed, but not too much to where I would start having conversations with toasters or something. I put the pipe down. I was ready to rub genitals with strangers.

I navigated my way toward the massive front door. I rang the fancy doorbell that sounded more like a song than just a sound. The pilot opened the door, leading me to his room. Sitting on the bed was who I assumed was the third guy. All I could think about was how awkward it must have been for the two of them to sit with each other waiting for me. They could have at least warmed up.

I didn't know what I expected the guy to look like, but that definitely wasn't it. He was tiny but not just in a short way. He looked like he had some kind of body abnormality. His face was similar. He was like the one kid in a regular classroom that went to Special Ed but only for an hour a week. You could tell something was different about him, but you weren't quite sure what. And you were definitely not going to ask.

It didn't matter to me if he was special or not. The only thing that bothered me was how he was casually sitting on the bed watching T.V. The pilot jumped next to him, making them look like an old heterosexual couple watching Law and Order reruns.

I took off my shoes and joined them. The pilot must have been making good money, because his silky bed sheets covered a memory foam mattress; it was euphoric to the touch. Or maybe that was just the weed kicking in. I did start feeling relaxed, although it could have been because the mysterious third person was finally revealed to me.

The three of us watched T.V. Thankfully, it was not Law and Order. Instead, it was some Lindsay Lohan movie that I had never seen. Before I could ask, my thoughts were interrupted.

"So are we going to start?" The pilot asked us.

I couldn't think of a sexier way to commence the fondling of genitals.

First, the pilot and I took turns with the new guy. Then we started a train. To my surprise, it felt nothing like how it looked in the numerous porn videos I had watched in preparation. There was a lot more falling over and our rhythms were not syncing up. We looked like those physics marbles on desks that bounced back and forth with the middle one remaining still.

My mind started getting cloudy. I felt my thoughts wandering off. It was getting increasingly difficult to focus on the task when I could hear Lindsay Lohan in the background.

I laughed in the middle of the sex train. Then I giggled

about how I was laughing. Then I started losing my erection and, that too, made me laugh.

I decided to tag out for a minute. That was the ultimate perk of a threesome; I was able to sit out and come back in at my leisure. I laid back on the bed, allowing the silky sheets to conform to my body, while I tried to maintain my giggling. The two guys aggressively humped next to me.

On the T.V., Lindsay Lohan was at a new school making friends with a giant gay guy, a gothic (possible) lesbian, and a very bitchy blonde girl. I didn't have a clue what the plot was, but every few seconds a line would be said causing me to laugh. I tried to suppress the giggling.

I couldn't tell if it was a bad idea to have smoked before going in, or if it was a bad idea to have such an entertaining movie playing in the background—maybe a combination of both. As the two guys were banging each other's brains out practically on top of me, I stared at the T.V. wondering if Cady Heron was going to be successful in taking down The Plastics.

It felt like only seconds had passed but, when I looked over, the pilot was fully clothed and the other guy was gone.

"So, um, yeah…" The pilot mumbled.

"Oh," I replied. "Guess I should leave."

I fumbled putting my clothes back on while keeping an eye on the movie. This was the first time I hadn't bolted out of a person's room after sex but, to be fair, I didn't even realize the sex was over.

"We should do that again sometime," the pilot said.

"What's this movie called?" I asked.

"You've never seen it? It's Mean Girls."

The movie was nearing its climax way before I did, but I had to leave the sanctuary of the silky bed. I got in my car, still giggling to myself. I scraped the bowl one last time before smoking the ash. Then I drove around searching for the nearest fast-food. Thankfully, there was an In-N-Out close by.

I sat in the drive-through waiting for a double-double with animal fries. I logged onto Amazon searching for Mean Girls. In seven to ten business days I would find out if Regina George got what was coming to her.

DRAGULA PART II

I was lost. I had no idea how I got there. Everything around me appeared the same no matter which direction I turned. I was stranded in a labyrinth of fabric.

I was somewhere in the Downtown L.A. Fashion District. That, I was sure of but nothing more. Every street was aligned with nearly identical vendors selling fabric by the yard. Each street spilled into the next, creating a never-ending chain of identical shops. Even the alleyways sold fabric. The only thing that broke up the monotony was the scattered ladies selling churros or pupusas.

I coward in the center of it all. I felt the dense shops gawking at me—laughing at my innocence. I felt them closing in like High School kids initiating a fat freshman. This was no place for someone that lacked a sense of fashion. I was outnumbered. I was stranded. I was helpless. I did the only thing I could do. I huddled into a corner next to a taco truck, hoping it was all just a dream.

"What are you doing, you weirdo?" Pinché's voice snapped me out of my fabric-fueled meltdown.

"Nothing…" I replied.

It was the end of September when the seasons were shifting. The dry, scorching heat season was transitioning into the dry, scorching heat with wind season. The day was finally cooling off reaching an eighty-five-degree low. We were sweating profusely in Santee Alley.

"What do you think of this one?" The Bear Queen asked, unrolling an unnecessarily long piece of fabric.

"Looks great," I said, as was my answer to that question every time. I couldn't tell the difference from one red to another. I especially couldn't tell the difference between what the fabrics felt like.

I was sure Pinché regretted inviting me to go shopping. I tried to stay as close to him as possible, like a child with a parent. He knew his way around the fabric maze. I feared that if he disappeared again, I'd be lost forever in the vortex of materials. I wasn't going to let him out of my sight even if it meant getting an education on the types of fabric I'd never remember.

Pinché continued running his hand up and down the aisles of fabric, searching for the perfect material. He had a specific idea of the outfit he wanted to make for the first episode of Dragula.

"It's the Boulet Brothers," Pinché said. "I've got to do something big every episode."

"What's the challenge for the first episode?" I asked.

"We're supposed to put together our best witch look."

"That's definitely different from mainstream drag," I mentioned.

He pulled out fabrics, and I nodded my head with approval to each one. Soon enough, he realized that I was completely useless. He would then just show me the ones he wanted me to approve of.

"I also have to figure out an outfit for the Halloween Ball," he said.

"Halloween ball?"

"Yeah, the Boulets throw a crazy Halloween event every year. This year is going to be a little different, though. They're going to have the Dragula competitors walk the runway before the episode airs."

"That actually sounds pretty fun."

"You better be coming," Pinché warned. "Everyone is going to be there."

"I don't know about that," I said, reluctantly. "I usually spend my exciting Halloween nights watching Netflix and falling asleep before ten."

"You have to come. Everyone is going to go all-out with insane costumes. It's so much fun."

"I haven't worn a costume since I was eleven."

"You don't dress up," Pinché said flatly.

"No," I replied.

"You don't dress up."

"No?"

"You're stupid. You're dressing up."

"I'm not comfortable enough with my body," I admitted. "Halloween costumes are generic sizes that aren't flattering on my small frame."

"Shut the hell up. Do you think my body type fits costumes? No, but I don't give a fuck. Besides, I make most of my own clothes anyway."

I had always envied Pinché's confidence. I couldn't remember the last time I'd seen him wear a shirt that wasn't see-through or revealing some part of his body. We had two completely different body types, but he was much more comfortable than I ever could be.

"I'll just make you a costume," Pinché continued.

"I couldn't ask for that. Especially not when you're this busy with Dragula," I told him.

"It will be easy. I'll just sew something up for you. What do you want to be?"

"It's okay. I'll just wear cat ears or something."

Pinché glared at me.

"Fine, I give up. There is one thing I've always wanted to dress up as. I want to look like a variation of the Goblin King from Labyrinth. David Bowie's character but more like an incarnation of a gothic god."

"Well, that was unexpected," Pinché said. "But we can

definitely do that."

"Like a leather cape with a towering collar. No sleeves so I can still show my tattoos. And, of course, tight pants to match Bowie's trademark bulge."

"I don't think there are tight enough pants to find your bulge," Pinché laughed. "I know exactly what to do."

The wheel of ideas was turning in Pinché's head. He darted out of the fabric shop, heading straight ahead to what appeared to be the exact same shop half a block away. I struggled to keep up but feared getting lost again.

"Like this for the cape?" Pinché asked, holding up a sturdy fabric.

My eyes lit up. "Yes!"

"And we can line the inside with this softer fabric so it's comfortable."

It was a fresh feeling being able to explain my idea to an artist and have them understand what I was talking about. Pinché understood my aesthetic and was going out of his way to help me embrace it. The excitement of getting a custom-made outfit for the biggest Halloween party in Downtown was incredible.

"You know you don't have to do this," I said, not knowing how to react when someone did something nice for me.

"I know. But I want to. I want you to be there and I want you to be comfortable. What do you want to wear under the jacket?"

"A T-shirt, I guess."

"Actually, it's going to be really hot in the venue. I'll probably just make it so you can be shirtless under the jacket.

"Hold up," I stopped him. "I can't be shirtless."

He rolled his eyes. "How about I make you a harness?"

We made a sharp turn into an accessory shop that was only slightly different than the rest of Santee Alley. He pulled a metal ring from a shelf along with a strap.

"The harness will give the costume some depth, and you won't be completely shirtless underneath," he continued.

"I admire your confidence," I told him. "But I don't think

I can do that."

"Just trust me," he said, seriously. "You're going to look amazing and you're going to be there with me, so you'll be comfortable."

I couldn't help but smile. Pinché's belief in himself was already inspiring but his confidence in me was even more so. I had someone that was positive I could pull off a look that I never thought I'd see myself in. The little queer kid was getting a costume made by a talented drag queen.

*   *   *

I was stuffing my face with street tacos from one of the trucks in Downtown, when my phone vibrated with a text message from Pinché. I shoved the rest of the tacos down my throat, hoping I wouldn't regret it later, and jumped into my car. I weaved in and out of traffic, dodging parked cars and homeless people.

Pinché had spent the day filming the first episode of Dragula. The anticipation was burning a hole in my mind as I conjured up as many possible scenarios as I could. I pulled up to Precinct where they were filming. Pinché lugged himself into my car, letting out a sigh.

"What happened?! Did you win yet? Who else is on it?" I asked before he could even close the door.

"Chill. I'm exhausted," he said without the usual pep in his voice.

"Well?"

"A bunch of local queens are on it: Meatball, Vander Von Odd, Loris, Frankie Doom. They had me shook when they brought out Melissa BeFierce."

"Who?"

"Melissa. He's like a drag sister to me. He's a really well-known WeHo queen. We were all surprised to see him in Downtown."

I pulled up to a stoplight, turning to Pinché. It was the first time I looked at him since he got in the car. His face was completely covered in glittery, black makeup. Even through it, I could see the exhaustion in his eyes from the day of filming, juggling regular gigs, and preparing for the episode.

"How did the runway go?" I asked.

"Well, I thought it went great until the judges read me to filth."

"I'm sure it wasn't that bad."

"Some people had really basic witch outfits. Some looked like Halloween costumes rather than drag. I tried to go for something different, but I guess it didn't translate."

"It's just the first episode. You'll be fine."

"I'm in the bottom three on the first episode."

"Oh," I said, taken aback. "That's not all bad. You'll at least get more camera time doing the extermination challenge."

The extermination challenge was the Boulets' way to determine who would be eliminated. The queens that did the weakest in the runway challenge would be sent to the extermination challenge to battle head-to-head. It was the equivalent to a "lip sync for your life" challenge except, instead of an actual lip sync, it would be more of a stunt. I had faith that Pinché was going to excel in whatever the stunt was going to be. There was no way he was going to be eliminated first.

"I wonder if the extermination challenge is going to be an actual challenge where the first person to reach the goal wins, or will it be completely subjective, like the lip sync in Drag Race?" I asked.

"I have no idea," Pinché replied. "But I'm going up against Loris and Meatball."

"Are you serious? You and Meatball are best friends."

"Yeah. It's going to be rough, but I came here to win."

Later that night, I drove my car beneath the light pollution of the city. I punched the gas up a winding street through the hills of Silver Lake. I reached the top, cautious not to bump into any oncoming cars on the single-lane street. It was eerily quiet compared to the hustle of the boulevard below.

Pinché was filming the extermination challenge in the area. He had only a few hours to prepare for the shoot. I loitered in my car with my foot on the brake to avoid rolling back down the steep hill. Thirty minutes passed by with my phone unable to grasp any kind of reception. I was trapped with my thoughts, once again speculating all the possible scenarios of the Dragula outcome.

The silhouette of a figure peeked from behind an overgrown bush. The shadowy figure emerged with a glittery body shimmering beneath the hazy sky.

Pinché opened the car door. The light struck him just enough for me to see his makeup running down, dirt covering his body, and plenty of other unknown substances staining his outfit.

"Is this from the challenge or just the long day?" I asked.

"Both," he replied.

"How'd it go?"

"Meh."

His chest hairs were matted with dirt. A tiny bug crawled across his skin, trying to burrow.

"Um, you got something—" I pointed.

He casually wiped the creature from his body. He slumped into the passenger seat, exhaling a giant breath.

"So…?" I kept trying to pry an answer.

"I think it went great," he finally replied. "They buried us in a coffin. Then we were covered with dirt. Had some crickets and maggots dumped on my face. Oh, and I almost drowned."

"That explains some things," I said, wiping dirt off his arm.

"I could hear the whole film crew laughing while I screamed in the coffin. So I think it went well. They were pretty silent when Loris got buried. It was fun though. They even interviewed me right after, asking how I felt. While I was telling them, a cricket hopped on me. So I ate it."

"Ew, you ate a cricket?"

"It's not the worst thing I've put in my mouth."

"That's probably true. So are you eliminated or not?"

"They're going to call me by the end of the night to let me know."

"Great. More waiting."

Pinché fell asleep almost immediately after I stopped

grilling him with questions. I was witnessing firsthand the amount of work he was putting into his career. Seeing him take advantage of the brief moment of rest really attributed to his dedication.

"Oh, shit!" Pinché bolted up out of his slumber. "I got to pick up my stuff from Vander's place tomorrow!"

"Maybe you should just get some rest tonight and not worry about that," I suggested. "If you weren't so tired, I would offer to take you now."

"There's no way I'm getting any sleep when I get home. There's way too much going through my mind right now."

I didn't doubt that. He couldn't even commit to napping in the car without thinking about what he had to do the next day. Despite being only a few streets away from his apartment, I turned the car around and cruised toward the freeway.

As if his power nap was enough to make up for a week's worth of sleep deprivation, Pinché finally offered me the rundown of the Dragula episode.

"There's this queen, Loris, that claimed to be vegan but wore leather, so I called him out on that in front of everyone. Melissa BeFierce—the one I told you about—slayed as always, but seemed a bit out of place in the competition. Ursula is definitely the favorite to win since he's performed for the Boulet Brothers the most. But I don't want to spoil too much for you."

"Spoil it all! Please!" I was dying to know everything. "Tell me all the drama."

"Actually, there wasn't a lot of drama."

"How is that possible with drag queens?" I questioned.

"I mean, there was nothing petty. All the queens on the show have worked with each other at some point or another. And we're going to have to continue to work together in L.A. after Dragula is over, so it wouldn't be good for us to fight with each other."

"I guess," I said, disappointed. "Who won the first challenge?"

"I don't know if I should—"

"Tell me!"

"Vander won the first challenge and it was very well-deserved."

I had never seen Vander Von Odd perform, but I had seen him in drag before. His makeup always seemed more of a special-effects style of art rather than traditional drag queen, but it seemed perfect for the concept of Dragula.

We pulled up to Vander's place. With the last of his energy, Pinché slid out of the car to embrace his drag sister. Vander had the same expression on his face that Pinché had earlier when I picked him up. These queens—these humans—hadn't gotten any rest over the last few weeks. It was clear that all their time was being dedicated to their art.

The two performers were on opposite ends of the competition spectrum—Pinché being in the bottom while Vander won the challenge. But outside of the drag world, they were two friends that had the most love and respect for one another.

"Congratulations on the victory," I said to Vander as he reached into the car to exchange a hug.

Pinché grabbed what he needed and returned to the car. We pulled away waving back to the challenge winner, hoping that the two queens would meet again on the next episode.

We trekked all the way back to Pinché's apartment. I was exhausted but wasn't about to complain.

"Thanks for driving," the Bear Queen said.

"No problem," I replied. "Let me know when the Boulets call you."

I watched as the weary queen lugged his bags toward the front steps. I was proud of him. I hoped he would get a good night's sleep before preparing for the next episode. I couldn't wait to see what Dragula would do for his career.

I pulled away from the apartment. Before I could reach the end of the street, my phone lit up.

"I'm eliminated," Pinché said.

"I'm so sorry," I responded, unsure of what else to say. "Are you okay?"

"I'm not good enough."

"What? I know this sucks, but it doesn't mean you're not

good enough."

"This was everything to me." His voice held back tears. "All my hard work has been for nothing. I am nothing. I've never fit in anywhere in my life until I started drag. Even now, I'm rejected by the Downtown community—the community I helped build. I'm not even good enough for the people I consider family."

"Do you want to spend the night?" I offered. "I can come pick you up again."

"No. I need to be left alone."

BELLE OF THE BALL

I woke up with the excitement of a kid on Christmas morning. Except it wasn't Christmas. It was Halloween. And I wasn't a kid. I was the spokesman for recreational Adderall. I was also teetering on the brink of functioning alcoholic and good old-fashioned millennial alcoholic that just referred to every drink as "brunch". Regardless, I was excited for that night's festivities.

The Boulet Brothers' Halloween Ball was already dominating my social media feed even more than "thoughts and prayers". It was what everyone in the underground drag scene was talking about, along with the subsequent premiere of Dragula. The Ball was going to be the last time we got to see all the queens together before the first episode would air.

It had been a couple weeks since Pinché's elimination. I hadn't seen him much during that time. Understandably, he was still disappointed with the result of the first episode. The feeling of rejection struck a nerve in him even deeper than I could have imagined. I gave him enough space to mull over everything that transpired but kept close enough to talk if he needed to.

His professional life was different, however. Nobody knew he was eliminated yet, and he used that to his advantage. Pinché was receiving offers to perform shows all over Los Angeles. He capitalized on being hot—booking as many gigs as he could before his elimination aired. Now on any drag show flyer, Pinché would be featured with the coveted title "from Dragula" above his picture.

The other queens on the show were benefitting just as much. The increase in regular drag shows headlined by Dragula queens was incredible. Almost overnight, the nine contestants were elevated into a spotlight even brighter than their previous fame. Their social media accounts were cluttering with followers from all over the country and beyond. They were becoming celebrities in our underground queer community right before our eyes.

It was with the announcement of Dragula, followed by the first promotional video, that Downtown Los Angeles solidified itself as an alternative queer community. We had our own celebrities, our own bars, and soon our own streaming drag show. DTLA welcomed all the queer people that didn't feel comfortable in WeHo or anywhere else. We no longer had to conform to the stereotypical ideas of what it meant to be gay just to fit in. We had a niche in Downtown and it was flourishing.

I could hardly contain my excitement. I texted Pinché before I even had my morning coffee, to tell him how excited I was. I didn't get a reply, but I wasn't surprised. I was sure he was busy preparing for the runway show he was going to be part of at the Ball.

I tried to calm myself down. I didn't want to get too excited and jump the gun by drinking way before it was time to. I had to avoid putting whiskey in my coffee for fear of becoming hungover by the time the sun set. Not that I had done that before, except I definitely had.

I got in the shower not knowing how many days it had been since my last one. That was just as good of an occasion as any to clean myself up. As the scalding water brought me tremendous joy, I could see my phone lighting up from beyond the shower doors. I reached out because, despite being soaking wet and full of suds, I felt the need to keep my phone close by.

It was a text from Pinché:

Sorry, I won't have your costume done.

I wiped my hands on a towel before replying:

How much of it did you finish? I'm sure it will be fine the way it is.

I stared at the phone as steam rose around me. I waited for the ellipses to appear on the screen indicating that Pinché was typing. The shower water ran cold before those three dots ever popped up.

I rushed through the rest of the shower before it got any colder. I dried my hair, threw on some lounging clothes, and made myself a jug of coffee. Then I checked my phone again. Still no reply.

Pinché had always shoved me out of my comfort zone. He elevated my confidence by believing in me. It was one of the kindest things someone had ever done for me when he offered to make my Halloween costume. He made me feel relevant not only by wanting me to attend the Ball, but also because he wanted to make the costume for me.

He finally texted back:

I don't have it.

My stomach fell with disappointment. I knew he was preoccupied with a lot of things, but just the night before he confirmed that the costume would be ready in time.

I loitered around my living room drinking copious amounts of black coffee and wondering why Pinché hadn't told me sooner that he wouldn't be done with the costume. I hoped he wasn't stuck in some kind of post-Dragula depression.

My body sank comfortably into my couch while Netflix sucked me into a vortex of binge watching Parks and

Recreation for the fifth time in my life. Hours raced by. Blankets and pillows were closing in on me. I didn't hear from Pinché again, and I had no costume to wear. There was only one logical conclusion to my day: there was no way I was leaving the couch.

After consuming enough coffee to give me the shakes, I had to balance out the caffeine. Naturally, I needed to drink an equal amount of liquor. I cracked open a fresh bottle of Jack Daniels and took a gulp every time Leslie Knope mentioned her love of whipped cream. With that, I was knocked out in no time.

When I finally regained consciousness, my phone lit up with a text message. I stretched over to see a picture of a cute guy with a crescent moon tattoo below his eye. Gabriel texted me:

Are you going to the Ball tonight? Would be cool to hang out.

I closed one eye to help me focus on the message. I texted back letting him know I was perfectly content with being absorbed into the couch. I had no intention of moving. He followed up by sending a picture of himself with just enough clothing to force me to want to see more. I folded:

Fine. I'll go.

Gabriel had become an exception to my ghosting rule. I enjoyed the casual dates we went on. He seemed like someone I could become close with. Usually when I noticed even a hint of feelings being developed for someone, I would escape as fast as I could. Gabriel was different.

I fought with gravity to tear myself away from the comfort of Netflix binging. I proceeded to get ready, throwing on a five dollar black shirt from the H&M clearance section and my only pair of jeans I washed once a month. Going out felt like a terrible idea, but I wanted to prove to myself that I didn't need to rely on a silly costume to make my night enjoyable. Also, meeting up with Gabriel sounded like a good idea, and I was sure Pinché would at least have time to have one drink with me.

I met up with Isadora in a dark parking lot in Downtown. I bought a "mini" bottle of Jack Daniels on the way. I pulled out an emergency stash of Adderall from my pocket and shoveled a mound of it into my nose.

"That doesn't seem like such a big deal," Isadora told me.

"It's not. It's a prescription drug," I assured him.

"Not that, stupid. The whole costume thing. And you're not even prescribed Adderall!"

"I didn't say it was my prescription." I took another bump. "It's not about the costume, though. It just sucks to get so close to someone then they suddenly distance themselves."

"It happens," Isadora said. "Let's just go in and have fun."

I finished the small bottle of whiskey and had razor-sharp focus from the drugs. My head was already pounding with a looming hangover from starting the debauchery too early. It probably didn't help that all I had to eat was a tortilla buried in my kitchen, that may or may not have had a bit of mold on it. Both my body and mind felt like they were already shutting down; like they were trying to tell me my night was over before it even began. Of course, I ignored them. Who needed food when they had drugs?

Isadora and I sashayed into the Boulet Brothers' Ball. The size of the Globe Theater was incredible. An impressive stage consumed half the main room, with a runway protruding into the dance floor. On the opposite side were tents with various drag queens hosting circus-like entertainment. Bookending the venue were two fully stocked bars that Isadora and I had the pleasure of racing toward.

After spending a wild amount of money on an overpriced cup of soda with a bit of liquor, we wandered around the venue. Everyone was dressed in elaborate costumes. People had prosthetic makeup, wide gowns, and creative looks. An authentic Nosferatu passed by us followed by a person on stilts. Everyone went all-out for the event.

As we were fighting our way across the dance floor, Pinché rushed past us. He had an elaborate costume of his own and looked to be making a beeline toward something. He nearly bumped into us but continued on his way.

"That was weird," I said.

"I don't think he noticed us," Isadora replied.

Isadora and I poked our heads into a couple of the tents to see what kind of entertainment our tickets were providing us. A group of people eagerly squeezed their way out of one of the tents.

"Wonder who's in there," I slurred at the Queen of Emotion.

We peeked in to find the always charming Meatball.

"Are you fuckers coming in or what?" He screeched.

"What are you doing in here?" I asked.

"I'm reading fortunes. What the hell does it look like I'm doing? Get in here. I'll read yours."

We obliged the boisterous queen mostly because we wanted him to stop yelling at us.

"Aye, qui, qui, qui,qui…." He began. "This one is hard to read, but I predict you guys will drink too much and regret it in the morning."

"Way ahead of you." I raised my drink. "Are you reading fortunes all night?"

"All right, your time is up. Get out of my tent. Next!" Meatball yelled followed by his cackle that made you unsure if he was joking or not.

We exited the humid tent to find that the venue was filling up. We made our way toward the patio for some fresh cigarette air when Pinché marched past us again.

"Hey!" I stopped the Bear Queen.

"Oh, hi," Pinché said to us.

"Where have you been?"

"Just busy," he replied, looking away. "I got to go."

As he walked away from us, Isadora turned to me. "Now, that was weird."

I agreed disappointedly. I was looking forward to hanging out with Pinché even just for a minute.

We finally found the sanctuary of the outside where only cigarette smoke could fit between each person. The patio was just as crowded as the inside and somehow even more sweaty.

I finished my cup of barely alcohol. I could smell my brain cells melting in a fiery inferno. My inhibitions were exploding like fireworks. The amount of alcohol, drugs, and disappointment coursing through my soul was shutting down any brain functionality I may have had left. My body continued moving—continued drinking—but my mind was gone. I passed the threshold of drinking to get drunk and entered the dark area of drinking to suffocate the thoughts in my head.

"There you are," a voice floated toward me.

I turned around to see Edward Scissor Hands. He gave me a hug, trying to maneuver his scissor hands around me.

"I've been looking for you," he continued.

I stared at him, unsure of who exactly he was. In L.A., it was common for me to be introduced to the same person at least three times before I remembered them. In the gay community, it was common to meet someone at least ten times before I remembered to stop saying "nice to meet you". Then in the drag community, I couldn't recognize a drag queen in their boy form to save my life. Now, I had to deal with trying to remember who that person was in a costume.

He clearly knew who I was, so I rolled with it.

"I think I need another drink," I said as an exit strategy.

"I'll go with you," the Edward negated my attempt.

"You guys go ahead. I'm going to finish this cigarette," Isadora said. "You okay?"

"Fine. Just one more drink," I told him.

The Edward and I made our way back into the packed venue. It was nearly impossible to pass the wall of pads and wigs of the usual drag queens. That night was even more difficult trying to pass non-performers with fairy wings and other spacious outfits. I would have sobered up (metaphorically) if we waited in line for the bar, so we ventured to find the restroom instead.

"Whoever put stairs to the restroom at a venue with drag queens is the devil," I shouted, trying to carefully maneuver myself down the steps.

We made it down in one piece, turning the corner to find

an entire room that we didn't know existed. There was a dance floor equipped with its own DJ and a bar. The floor was empty aside from us and a handful of other people trying to avoid the crowd upstairs. The bartender looked bored out of her mind. My eyes lit up at the prospect of giving her something to do.

"We're definitely staying down here," I told the Edward.

"Sounds good to me. I'm glad we finally get to hang out again."

Like a Jimmy Neutron brain blast, my mind exploded with the realization of who Edward was. It was dark in the Globe Theater aside from the blinding strobe lights and, more importantly, my vision was obscured by my friend Jack Daniels. At least my mind could finally put together who that person was.

"That's who you are!" I blurted.

I had completely forgotten why I even decided to go to the Ball. I searched for the tattoo of the crescent moon below his eye, but his face was covered with so much makeup and fake scars that I couldn't quite make out the trademark ink.

"Huh?" The Edward asked.

"Nothing. Let's take shots."

"Jaeger?"

Nothing in the world sounded like a worse idea than taking a shot of Jaeger.

"Let's do it."

We took more than a couple shots of the black licorice-flavored syrup. We drank so much that dancing sounded like a good idea. We took the floor to ourselves in the empty room. I felt like we could have won Dancing With the Stars but, in retrospect, we probably looked like two fumbling teenagers at a middle school dance.

As our bodies got closer, I could feel his junk press against my leg. I couldn't help but think of the irony if Edward Scissor Hands was uncut.

Our faces got closer. Our dancing got heavier. Then, I either started to pass out on his face or I kissed him. Either way, our mouths connected. We exchanged Jaeger-flavored saliva in the center of the dance floor, no doubt making the DJ

and bartender sick. Everyone's discomfort—including my own
—was off the charts.

"I got to piss," I announced with class.

I moved away from the Edward, toward the restroom. I
was unsure if I had to urinate or puke or possibly both. On the
way to the toilet, I made eye contact with a guy that had
perfectly coiffed hair. He was dressed as a pirate with an
adorable dimple below his eyepatch.

"Hey," the pirate said, smiling excitedly.

"Hi," I responded, confused why an attractive stranger
would attempt to talk to me.

I moved toward the restroom. When I came back out, the
pirate was still staring at me.

"So, you're just going to ignore me?" He asked.

"Um, what?"

Annoyed, he lifted his eyepatch so I could take in the full
effect of his glare. A tiny crescent moon tattoo rested below
his right eye. "Forget it," he pouted, turning away.

It hit me like an extremely cliché Halloween episode
where the character gets confused by the person they're with
because of their costume. I had spent the entire night hanging
out with a person I thought was Gabriel.

I tried to stop the pirate—the real Gabriel—but he
disappeared into a crowd of people. I went back to the empty
dance floor where Edward Scissor Hands was looking down at
his phone.

"Holy balls," I said to myself. "Who is that then?"

I turned around before he could notice me struggling to
figure out who he was. I climbed the inconvenient staircase
back to the main room. It was finally clear to me that I was
beyond blacked out enough. I made an Irish exit to avoid the
consequences of my poor decisions. I stumbled through the
Globe Theater—past a scary witch, a scary dead cheerleader,
and an even scarier Rubella Spreads. I managed to find the exit,
leaving the Boulet Brothers' Ball behind me.

I ran across Broadway avoiding a horde of people and
speeding cars. I found a comfortable alley that only smelled
slightly of stale piss. I focused intensely on ordering a Lyft

from my phone. Unsurprisingly, the ride-share app had an unholy surge in price.

"Fuck!" I yelled with all the frustration of the night boiling over. "Fuck you!"

I smashed my phone onto the ground, obliterating it. It exploded like a volcano of tiny plastic pieces.

My heart raced. My adrenaline was pumping. The Adderall and alcohol had my body shaking. It was impossible to calm down. I started running. I ran down 8th Street. My Doc Martens clomped over the uneven pavement. I was seven miles away from my apartment. I didn't care that it was the middle of the night. I didn't care that I was alone in Downtown L.A. I was angry with myself for relying on Pinché. I was angry for allowing myself to get close to someone that was now distancing themselves from me. I was angry that I wasted my night with a person that I didn't even know, instead of being with the person I wanted to be with. I was angry that I drank so much and even more angry that I consumed so much amphetamine.

I stopped running, unable to breathe. I was near the freeway and didn't know what else to do. I had no way of calling a Lyft or anyone else to pick me up. So I stuck out my thumb toward the cars passing by me. The headlights were blinding. I hoped someone would pick me up. A few cars slowed down but still passed me. I didn't really think anyone would stop because it was the twenty-first century and nobody hitchhiked anymore. At least not in L.A.

"Hey, you all right?" A security guard from a nearby parking lot asked.

"Fantastic," I replied through gritted teeth.

I kept forcing my shaking legs toward the freeway with my thumb out. Finally, a car pulled up in front of me. It was a fancy suburban SUV. No words were exchanged before the driver opened the passenger door. I had to leap up to reach the seat.

The heater was comforting. Even the seat had its own warmer. I didn't look directly at the person driving. They could have been anywhere from a tall, old black man to a young, white frat guy. I wouldn't have noticed a difference at that point. All I knew was that it was a man.

"Where you going?" He asked, pulling away from the curb.

"Anywhere in Hollywood."

The rush I got from the fear of not knowing that person was intense. The potential danger was more of a high than the Adderall or whiskey. Sure, I had taken plenty of Lyfts before, but this was not a car registered on an app. There was no GPS tracker. I didn't even have a phone to call for help if I needed it.

I kept my hands in my pockets to try to hide my shaking.

"You have a knife?" The stranger asked.

"No," I replied.

"You sure?"

"Yes."

"It seems like you have a knife."

"Look, asshole, if you don't want to drive me then just leave me here."

The driver pulled over without hesitation. He unloaded me somewhere on Santa Monica Boulevard. Thankfully, I was much closer to my apartment than before but still miles away. I stuck my thumb out again.

In a shorter amount of time than before, a truck pulled over in front of me. The vehicle was beat up, carrying various tools in its flatbed. I got into the truck. Again, the driver could have been the size of a sumo wrestler or a dwarf, I wouldn't have noticed either way.

We headed west on Santa Monica for a couple miles when we came close to my street.

"You can just drop me off here," I pointed at the upcoming 7-Eleven just before Highland.

The stranger drove past the convenient store. I could feel myself sweating despite the cold night.

"You passed the spot," I told him.

He kept driving.

My eyes widened. Buildings rapidly passed me. I gripped the door handle, ready to jump out if an opportunity presented itself. Finally, the truck slowed down for a stoplight. But before he could reach it, the stranger turned the car into a hidden parking lot. He pulled into a parking space behind a low hanging tree branch, cutting the engine off. I pulled on the door handle, but it didn't budge.

The stranger grabbed his crotch. "So, you going to suck my dick?"

"No," I responded. I tried the door once more. It didn't move.

I refused to place a stranger's genitals into my mouth in exchange for a ride. However, I felt guilty for having nothing to offer him for his service. I also desperately needed to get out of that truck, and he was waiting for some sort of payment.

"You can suck mine," I told him.

I unzipped my skinny jeans. My penis flopped out in a drunken mess. His face attacked my lap. His head bobbed up and down.

After a minute of listening to the sound of the stranger gagging, I was bored and felt like I fulfilled my end of the unspoken bargain. I pulled him off of me. I zipped up my pants, put my hand on the door handle, and charged it with my shoulder. The door swung open. I caught myself before I could fall.

I ran back toward 7-Eleven. I brushed past the homeless LGBT youth that hung out in the area. I raced the few blocks to my apartment. I struggled to keep my legs moving, but all I could think about was filing that night away as a distant memory.

I fumbled with my keys, trying to open the door to my apartment building. I dropped them onto the cold concrete. I reached down seeing multiple sets of keys but trying to pick the one that was actually there. I rushed to open the door, fearing the stranger followed me home. Finally, the door opened.

I stepped toward the elevator. As soon as it opened, I shifted inside and collapsed onto the floor. My body had been on autopilot for the last few hours. Now it recognized I was home and no longer needed to function. I reached up to press the fourth floor button.

The elevator stopped on my level. I peeled myself off the sticky floor with immense effort. I carried myself a few more feet to my front door. Thankfully, I got it open with one try.

I slammed the door behind me.

My eyes crossed. My head swayed. There was a sharp pain creeping up my neck into the back of my head. My stomach churned. A stream of vomit launched in front of me, splattering onto the floor. The spew of Jack Daniels and Jaegermeister looked like airborne sludge. My entire body followed it. I slumped face-first into the pool of my stomach fluids.

I was woken up hours later by the sound of my teeth chattering and the warmth of blood dripping out of my nose. My body was violently shivering. Sweat was pouring from my face and all over my body. I struggled to inhale air into my tight chest. My stomach twisted causing me to gag, but nothing came out. I kept dry heaving, unable to breathe.

With maximum effort, I pulled myself off the floor, took two steps, and fell again. I laid there shaking. Sweating. Gagging. Bleeding. I hoped that death wouldn't take over. I also hoped that it would.

DRAGCON

Months went by since Pinché and I had spoken.

A cold distance was forming between us for reasons I was unsure of. I tried to talk to him a few times after Halloween but got no response. Part of me believed that Pinché was still recovering from his elimination from Dragula. Another part of me wondered if I had done something wrong.

Dragula finally aired. The viewership for the first episode reached over a hundred thousand views and each episode after that gained even more. The Downtown community was obsessing over the new show. People across America were tuning in. The contestants were gaining international fans. Dragula was blowing up!

The show was an instant success, proving that there were people in the world ready for an alternative to mainstream drag. People were interested in queens that spewed blood, wrestled each other, and shoved rosaries up their rectums. The evolution of mainstream drag enabled subcultures to branch out, and the queer community was ready for it.

Having a global audience engaged with the first episode of Dragula meant that hundreds of thousands of people had seen Pinché get eliminated first. Regardless, it was an impressive feat to be a part of something so new and successful. Pinché Queen was the dream of a small-town queer kid that made his way to Los Angeles. He helped shape a community that promoted the acceptance of all LGBT+ people that didn't feel like they fit in anywhere else.

After what turned out to be alcohol poisoning and a near overdose at the Boulet Brothers' Halloween Ball, I was too ashamed of myself to engage in any kind of delinquency. I pulled back on drinking and quit drugs altogether. I stopped going to drag shows. I avoided social media. I developed a routine of going to the gym, drinking pressed juices, and going on long hikes. I was one meditation class short of feeling like a true Angeleno—trying to avoid any kind of real feelings by focusing on staying active.

The winter months were long, lonely, and terribly boring. I still hung out with Isadora and Jessica, occasionally. Isadora's fanbase continued growing with his steady booking of gigs since the Wepa competition. Despite not being crowned the winner, he was on the DTLA radar.

Jessica was still very much the social media god of drag queens. As an attendee of most shows, she promoted the queens and kept social media colorful and queer.

"You have to start coming back out," Jessica told me. "It's been way too long since I've seen your dumb face."

"I'm not sure…" I said, reluctantly.

"Are you at least coming to DragCon?"

"Doubt it. I've never even been."

"You have to come this year. Dragula is going to have a panel with all the queens, and they're expected to make some announcements."

It had been less than a year since I was introduced into the world of DTLA's underground drag. It was a tumultuous year full of near-death experiences, self-discovery, and genuine happiness. I owed it to myself to commemorate it all. I had to attend L.A.'s DragCon to see the Dragula queens reunite one last time.

*　　　　　*　　　　　*

I woke up the earliest I had ever woken up for a drag event. DragCon opened at the unholy hour of 10 a.m. My heart was racing while I got ready, but that could have been from the copious amounts of coffee I had just consumed.

I arrived at the Convention Center in Downtown not long after. I wandered around outside while I waited for Jessica. The disgustingly delicious aroma of bacon-wrapped hotdogs permeated my nose. Dozens of food carts strategically surrounded the area, and each one was crowded with hungry homos, despite everyone knowing it was a trap to eat street meat.

Even though I was fully aware of the regret that would follow eating the greasy delectable, I found myself inching closer and closer to a vendor. My ability to resist was getting weaker. Then a beam of sunlight ripped through the smog in the distance, illuminating a mystical creature. The reflection of bright purple could only mean one thing. Like a guardian angel to my bowel movements, Jessica waddled her way toward me.

"Finally!" I shouted at the cock-blocker.

"Calm your tits. You're lucky I even got up this early," Jessica spat, shaking the sweat out of her floral Vander Von Odd T-shirt.

"Let's go in before I make a bad decision."

We made our way into the Convention Center. We navigated through a line of people, metal detectors, and an excruciatingly long hallway. The building smelled like stuffy politics. The floors were carpeted with an awful green color typically reserved for a grandmother's house. It seemed like the last place a homosexual—or anyone with a personality—would be found in. It was unfabulous to say the least.

We entered through a row of open doors. My Doc Martens landed on the fuzzy pink carpet that greeted us. I stared at two hundred thousand square feet of the most colorful people I had ever seen. The majority of them were drag queens, but I was surprised to see who the rest of the population was comprised of.

There was a middle-aged white man in a suit wearing high heels, racing past us. There was a group of High School kids in the corner putting on nail polish. Heterosexual parents held hands with their son while he wore a dress. A cholo had his arm around his girlfriend's waist as she sported a Trixie Mattel T-shirt.

It was strange, yet empowering, to see the regular daytime world merge with the pageantry of a nighttime art. I had never thought how drag performances only took place at bars, making it impossible for anyone under eighteen to see a show unless it was on T.V. But during that day, young fans and other people that we didn't normally see at bars, were able to experience everything drag had to offer.

Tall, chubby drag queens towered above vendors. Short, muscular queens wore hair doubling their height. There were queens wearing classic dresses and queens in elaborate costumes. Ru girls like Trinity the Tuck, Morgan McMichaels, and Farrah Moan wandered around the pink carpet. New queens trying drag for the first time were sharing the same area.

Every type of style and experience was represented— everyone except the underground queens of Downtown L.A. All the attendees were polished and beautiful. Their wigs were perfectly styled; their nails were colorfully painted.

I looked down at my boots. My black jeans were as tight as a drag queen's tuck. I wore a cutoff shirt that read "Sad As Fuck". My face tattoo glimmered beneath the bright lights. I already felt out of place standing at the entrance.

"Jessica!" A shrill voice shouted toward the Grimace impersonator.

"Frankie!" She shouted back.

The colossal queen with a body nearly hidden behind a teased, multi-colored wig, bent down to wrap his arms around Jessica. Frankie Doom's breastplate rested on top of her head as they embraced. Among all the traditional queens at the convention, it was comforting to see a monster like Frankie.

Coming off of making it to the finale of Dragula, Frankie was in high demand and had to continue making his rounds around DragCon. Jessica and I finally stepped off the pink carpet, ready to see what the convention had to offer.

"I think Dakota D'vil has a booth somewhere," Jessica said. "All the Downtown queens will be there."

We weaved and slipped through the crowd as best as we could, finally finding fresh air in a far aisle.

"Oh my god, Jessica!" A voice danced through the air. Valerie Von Boom came up to us. "Here, take some of these. We're promoting our event at CFrenz. Have some free drink vouchers."

"I already drink for free there," Jessica replied before handing me all of the tickets.

"I'm loving DragCon already," I smiled.

We continued our journey passing all types of vendors: clothing, leather goods, jock straps, makeup. We pushed through a crowd of people waiting in a long, exclusive line that led toward a private area where RuPaul was signing autographs.

"This place is—Oh, shit!" I blurted, trying to hide my face.

Jessica looked around. "What is it?"

"That guy over there," I said, concealing my face in Jessica's shoulder. "He's insane and has texted me every day for the last eight months. I've never even replied."

"Is this another person you slept with?"

"You say that as if this happens often."

"Every time we go out!" Jessica informed me. "You say you can't go into certain bars because you messed around with someone that works there, or you hide in the corner trying to avoid people."

"I do not!" I rebutted.

"I bet I know exactly what your cycle is. You make someone feel real special and act like you're interested in them. Then you give them a mediocre dick down—just enough to make them want to do it again. Then you ghost the poor insecure person, making them think they did something wrong and you're on to the next one."

"Actually… Wait. Did you say 'mediocre dick down'?"

"Mediocre at best," she confirmed.

"Im not going to agree, but I'm also not going to disagree."

We continued along the perimeter of the convention, trying to stay safe from rogue shoulder pads and sharp heels. We peeked down each aisle to see if we could find Dakota's booth, but there were so many that it could have taken all day to find him.

"Oh my god!" Screeched a young guy that was very obviously in drag for the first time. "Are you Jessica?"

"Hey! How are you?!" Jessica replied, ecstatically.

"Oh my god, I follow you on Instagram! I love you so much!"

Usually people fangirl over drag queens, but this person was happy to meet the unofficial social media promoter that uploaded drag videos. The amateur queen even had a photo-op with Jessica.

"You have no idea who that was, do you?" I asked when the fan was far enough away.

"Not a clue," Jessica replied.

"I swear, you're more famous than most of these drag queens."

"It's tough being famous." She flipped her purple hair back.

We passed a couple booths of artists selling their respective brands of clothing. Black Mast—a San Francisco based company—had a prominent booth showing off their original T-shirt designs.

Sissy Boy clothing also had a spot. I fell in love with their name immediately. With such an offensive slur used as a brand name, I couldn't help but obsess over how taboo it was. Despite Jessica's complaints of needing to sit down, I forced her to come with me to buy merchandise.

"Jessica," another voice from behind us shouted.

"Someone else you know?" I asked. I was getting jealous of how many people knew her. "How do I not know anyone here?"

We moseyed over to the booth that was calling her name. Jessica greeted Mariah Balenciaga. Before he went back to signing autographs, he offered Jessica a chair.

"It blows my mind that everyone here goes up to drag queens, but the drag queens come up to you," I said to Jessica.

"I am the superior fag hag," she replied. "You cool with hanging here for a bit? My tired ass needs to rest."

"I'm going to keep roaming—see what kind of trouble I can get into."

We had only covered a third of the Convention Center, but it felt like we had already walked for miles. I went up and down a few more avenues by myself. My anxiety was building an immunity to large queer crowds, and I was getting used to dodging shopping bags and ducking beneath wigs.

I passed a few familiar booths. One of them was for club sCum—the most queer-punk event in East L.A. I was thrilled to finally see a booth that represented the underground drag scene. I rummaged through their T-shirts and pins until I heard a voice call from behind me.

"Oh, there's the one that plays too much!" The voice blared from across multiple aisles. Despite the dull roar of the crowded Center, the voice cut through the air like a neurotic termite through wood.

"Hi, Cake Moss," I said, wishing I could disappear. Every person that Jessica ran into was tranquil and a pleasure to meet. The one person that I ran into had to be Cake Moss.

Cake whipped his braided wig around as he glided up to me on roller skates. He stopped merely inches from my face. The stench of cheap weed and genitalia burned the air as he cracked his tongue.

"Don't act cute with me. I ain't going to be chasin' after you. You ain't getting none of this," he said, twirling on his skates.

"Okay," I replied.

"What are you doing tonight?" He cracked his tongue again.

"I'm busy."

"Are you going to invite me over or what?"

"Um, no."

"I can ride my bike to you."

"No."

"Why you always playin'?!"

Just as he was about to burst into a tirade, an adorable hispanic guy came up to Cake, exchanging a hug. He was very clean-cut wearing a polo shirt and designer jeans.

"Man, this is nothing like L.A. Pride," the guy told Cake.

"I know. There is not enough booty up in this bitch," Cake replied. "Downtown is whack."

"Nobody is drunk and I wore my cock ring for nothing."

Cake Moss was a very prominent drag queen in WeHo, and his friend was clearly from the same area. DragCon was nothing like Los Angeles Pride for all the right reasons. The Downtown event catered to everyone, rather than just to entitled gay males obsessing over copious amounts of alcohol and partying.

My eyes were opened to the reality that I used to be one of those people. I had spent my adult life jumping from bar to bar, being content with blacking out multiple times a week and shoveling an endless amount of drugs into my face. I had never cared about the Stonewall riots, the AIDS epidemic, or the queer political powers that fought for everything our community gained. All I had cared about was being intoxicated.

That changed as I grew comfortable with the Downtown L.A. community. Of course, there was still drinking and partying, but that became secondary compared to everything else the DTLA community was offering. I had never been surrounded by so many artists in my life. The community boasted people trying to inspire others. Besides the drag queens, there were queer people creating their own clothing lines, opening LGBT+ businesses, and making names for themselves with artwork of various mediums.

LGBT+ culture and history was being recognized in Downtown; it was being celebrated. Every letter beneath the LGBT+ umbrella was flourishing, unlike the cis-male domination of WeHo. The queer community was changing, and I was changing with it.

I was ready to put away the week-long binges and passing

out in alleys. I wanted more from myself and from the people around me. I wanted to bask in the art more than the alcohol.

I was proud that the queer community was evolving. We had come a long way from when the only places we could hang out were in bars and bathhouses.

"You're right," I told the guy. "This is nothing like L.A. Pride. I've got to go. Sorry about your cock-ring situation."

I sped away before Cake Moss could respond.

I raced around trying to find Jessica again, because being by myself was clearly not working out for me. I headed toward the front of the convention when I saw a miniature bounce house in the shape of a castle. Around it was tiny plastic chairs, and tables full of coloring books. A massive sign stood proudly in front of the area that read: Drag Queen Story Hour.

Drag Queen Story Hour was an organization that brought Drag Queens to libraries across America to read to children. A few months prior, I had the privilege of accompanying Rubella Spreads to the Eagle Rock Public Library, where he had the opportunity to read to children.

When we entered the small room in the library, there was a table filled with children's books that celebrated LGBT+ families, gender fluidity, and queer people of color. Rubella was able to pick a few books that he wanted to read to the kids.

At first, there were only four kids that showed up. But, just before the event was about to begin, the room filled to capacity with children and their families. All the seats were taken leaving standing room only. Rubella read books like Worm Loves Worm, Be Who You Are, and Not All Princesses Dress In Pink. In between readings, he led the children in nursery rhymes.

It was heartwarming to see a queen take their art out of the bar and into a more powerful place. As I watched Rubella read to children, it made me look back on my childhood and wish that I had an event like that growing up—something that would have told me it was okay to be myself. Part of me was angry and jealous, but each generation of LGBT+ people had to leave the world a better place for the next ones. I was proud that my generation brought drag queens into the mainstream.

I continued my journey through DragCon when I saw flashes of purple peeking through the crowd.

"You ready to find Dakota's booth?" Jessica asked me.

"I'm starting to feel like it doesn't exist."

DragCon was nearing its end. Unlike any other event involving drag queens, this one was scheduled to end before sunset. Jessica and I power walked (or power waddled, as she called it) down a couple more avenues. Her legs were beginning to give up, and she needed a place to sit. I was right behind her with that sentiment.

Then we turned a corner.

Dakota D'vil lay across a table with his legs angled like a genderless rock god in tight leather pants. In his hand dangled a pair of headphones. He held them as if they contained the secret to everlasting orgasms and was daring anyone to listen.

"Dakota!" Jessica shouted with relief.

Behind the table, Puzzi was helping with the display of Dakota's new album and merchandise.

"There you are!" Puzzi called to Jessica. "We were wondering when you were going to be here. Come sit down, sit down."

Like the loving mother that Puzzi was, she made room for Jessica and me to rest, away from the crowd. Next to the booth was Saint Peter D'vil selling his fang necklace.

It was relieving to have finally found the booth that we were most comfortable at. DragCon was welcoming, but it was comforting to be home with our niche of people. As I was embracing the moment of relaxation, a familiar face came up to the booth.

Ali Doom wore strings and thread as clothing that didn't leave much to the imagination. She hung out at the booth, making it feel like a Whore Haus reunion.

"Vander!" Someone called out to a gleam of red glitter across the aisle.

Vander Von Odd, proudly wearing the Dragula crown he earned when he won the show, came over out of breath. Between meet-and-greets, panels, and other DragCon festivities, he was running around all weekend. Behind him was an older man and woman in casual clothes that looked out of place at the convention.

"Guys," Vander announced to us, "these are my parents."

We were all stunned. I couldn't imagine how fulfilling it must have been to have his parents not only support his drag, but to be there witnessing what it was like to build a name in the community. They looked like they were still registering the pageantry of the experience, but they were no doubt proud of their son.

Vander was the embodiment of dedication to art. Everything about his character—outfit, makeup, hair—was executed with tremendous detail. He had an innate ability to make everything elaborate. Vander was the perfect representative not only for the underground drag scene, but of the title of Dragula's Super Monster.

"Ooh, henny! My feet are wrecked!" Meatball's terrorizing voice blasted.

"You and me both," Pinché agreed, carrying a pizza toward the booth.

I hadn't seen Pinché in months, and I couldn't even remember the last time we spoke. I was unsure if I should say anything to him, or if we were going to completely ignore each other. He made his rounds hugging everyone at the booth. I braced myself for how awkward it was going to be when he skipped me in the circle; I hoped that nobody would notice.

He hugged Jessica. Then Puzzi. I took a deep breath accepting that he was going to pass me. Then Pinché turned and put his arm around me. Our bodies barely touched for less than a split second. It was the coldest hug I had ever received in my life. There was no emotion behind it. There wasn't even a genuine greeting. It was the same kind of hug he gave to anyone that came up to him after a show and complimented his drag.

It was cold and I loved it. I was just relieved we weren't going to be the kind of people that ignored each other's existence. We didn't have to be friends (for reasons I still wasn't sure of), but at least he was cordial. We were still part of the same DTLA queer family and treated each other with respect.

Time felt like it was standing still as I looked around at everyone at the booth. The D'vils, Ali Doom, the Dragula queens, Jessica, and Puzzi—it was like a who's who of the underground drag world.

The moment reminded me of Andy Warhol's Factory. All of Warhol's artist friends shared a space to hang out in. At the time, nobody knew how special it was to have them all in one place. Artists of that time were just making their respective art and enjoying each other's company. It was impossible for them to know just how iconic their stories would become.

As I looked around at the artists surrounding me, the majority of them were wearing Saint Peter's fang necklace—a symbol of the underground community. We were living through something special. These were the people who had no idea just how iconic their stories would become. They may have never received the proper accolades for their work, but it was those people that paved a way for the next generation of alternative drag queens. I had the privilege of witnessing the evolution of drag and nobody even knew it yet.

A loud CLACK ripped through the air. Isadora approached us with a massive fan cooling off his face. Behind him was an entourage of friends.

"Girl, it is hot in here!" The Queen of Emotion said.

It was only appropriate for Isadora to join me in that moment. If it hadn't been for him, I wouldn't have been introduced to the drag world. It was because of Isadora that I had finally found a group of people that I felt accepted in. For the first time in my life, I felt comfortable with who I was.

"Who's that with you?" I asked.

Behind Isadora was a twelve-year-old girl carrying a bag full of souvenirs.

"This is my niece," he said.

"You told your niece you do drag?" I asked with my mouth open.

"Of course. I'm her favorite queen. Well, besides Farrah. We just got his autograph."

I gave Isadora a hug before he left the convention. Vander continued on his way with his parents. Pinché and Meatball finished their pizza before leaving. Puzzi and Saint Peter helped Dakota pack up his merchandise.

"The last panel of the day is Dragula," Jessica informed me. "We should get to it before it starts."

Jessica and I waited in the line to the conference room where the Boulets were going to host their panel for Dragula. We found seats in the center behind Vander's parents. Within minutes, the entire room was filled with people. Every seat was taken, but that didn't discourage people from filing in. People found room on the floor, on each other's laps, and crammed against the wall.

The front of the room held a riser with chairs. The Boulet Brothers took their seats, followed by the nine contestants on either side of them. All the queens got an opportunity to discuss their opinions of the show and each other. At the end of the panel, the Boulets opened up the floor for questions from the audience.

A hand in the back of the room shot up. They rose out of their seat and asked, "What's next for Dragula?"

The Boulet Brothers exchanged a look.

"Dragula has been confirmed for a second season."

EPILOGUE

The state of the Downtown Los Angeles LGBT+ community is constantly evolving. Some drag queens have met an early retirement, sashaying into new ventures, while new drag queens have risen into the spotlight.

I've since had the privilege of making acquaintances with talents like Vicky Jean Mochi, Maebe A. Girl, Tony Berrow, Chloe Darling, Barbra Wyre, Kornbread Jeté, Erika Klash, among others.

I'm proud to be witnessing a rise in non-binary, trans, and cis women performers because, despite what some ultra famous queen might say, drag is for EVERYONE. Performers like Baby Blue, Joey Flamboyant, Skirt Cocaine, Clit Eatswood, Charles Galin, and others are breaking the glass ceiling.

DTLA Proud—the alternative to Los Angeles Pride—has become a staple of summertime pride festivals. It promotes inclusion of every letter under the LGBT+ umbrella, with a spotlight on people of color and women.

The Los Angeles LGBT Center's Anita May Rosenstein Campus has officially opened and offers affordable housing for seniors and one hundred beds for homeless youth.

Isadora's mom and sister have since attended his shows. They are both proud and finally understand what drag means to him.

Spoons has moved out of state. He still has an impressive amount of sex and, miraculously, has never contracted an STD.

Milo has fully transitioned into the man we always knew he was.

Jessica is still the supportive mother that every drag queen needs.

Pinché Queen and I casually speak. We never enter the same venue without greeting each other. I will always have a love for him as a person outside of drag, and I will always be a fan of his art.

Rubella Spreads is still obnoxious.

ABOUT THE AUTHOR

Born and raised in Los Angeles, California, London Alexander spends his time writing television comedy scripts, poetry, and memoirs. He prides himself as an amateur activist and an advocate for civil rights. He loves whiskey and balloon animals.

londonalexander.net